The Defense

by
Apuleius

Translated by H. E. Butler

For my part, Claudius Maximus, and you, gentlemen who sit beside him on the bench, I regarded it as a foregone conclusion that Sicinius Aemilianus would for sheer lack of any real ground for accusation cram his indictment with mere vulgar abuse; for the old rascal is notorious for his unscrupulous audacity, and, further, launched forth on his task of bringing me to trial in your court before he had given a thought to the line his prosecution should pursue. Now while the most innocent of men may be the victim of false accusation, only the criminal can have his guilt brought home to him. It is this thought that gives me special confidence, but I have further ground for self-congratulation in the fact that I have you for my judge on an occasion when it is my privilege to have the opportunity of clearing philosophy of the aspersions cast upon her by the uninstructed and of proving my own innocence. Nevertheless these false charges are on the face of them serious enough, and the suddenness with which they have been improvised makes them the more difficult to refute.

For you will remember that it is only four or five days since his advocates of malice prepense attacked me with slanderous accusations, and began to charge me with practice of the black art and with the murder of my step-son Pontianus. I was at the moment totally unprepared for such a charge, and was occupied in defending an action brought by the brothers Granius against my wife Pudentilla. I perceived that these charges were brought forward not so much in a serious spirit as to gratify my opponents' taste for wanton slander. I therefore straightway challenged them, not once only, but frequently and emphatically, to proceed with their accusation.

The result was that Aemilianus, perceiving that you, Maximus, not to speak of others, were strongly moved by what had occurred, and that his words had created a serious scandal, began to be alarmed and to seek for some safe refuge from the consequences of his rashness.

Therefore as soon as he was compelled to set his name to the indictment, he conveniently forgot Pontianus, his own brother's son, of whose death he had been continually accusing me only a few days previously. He made absolutely no mention of the death of his young kinsman; he abandoned this most serious charge, but — to avoid the appearance of having totally abandoned his mendacious accusations — he selected, as the sole support of his indictment, the charge of magic — a charge with which it is easy to create a prejudice against the accused, but which it is hard to prove.

Even that he had not the courage to do openly in his own person, but a day later presented the indictment in the name of my step-son, Sicinius Pudens, a mere boy, adding that he appeared as his representative. This is a new method. He attacks me through the agency of a third person, whose tender age he employs to shield his unworthy self against a charge of false accusation. You, Maximus, with great acuteness saw through his designs and ordered him to renew his original accusation in person. In spite of his promise to comply, he cannot be induced to come to close quarters, but actually defies your authority and continues to skirmish at long range with his false accusations. He persistently shirks the perilous task of a direct attack, and perseveres in his assumption of the safe role of the accuser's legal representative. As a result, even before the case came into court, the real nature of the accusation became obvious to the meanest understanding. The man who invented the charge and was the first to utter it had not the courage to take the responsibility for it. Moreover the man in question is Sicinius Aemilianus, who, if he had discovered any true charge against me, would scarcely have been so backward in accusing a stranger of so many serious crimes, seeing that he falsely asserted his own uncle's will to be a forgery although he knew it to be genuine: indeed he maintained this assertion with such obstinate violence, that even after that distinguished senator, Lollius Urbicus, in accordance with the decision of the distinguished consulars, his assessors, had declared the will to be genuine and duly proven, he continued — such was his mad fury — in defiance of the award given by the voice of that most distinguished citizen, to assert with oaths that the will was a forgery. It was only with difficulty that Lollius Urbicus refrained from making him suffer for it.

I rely, Maximus, on your sense of justice and on my own innocence, but I hope that in this trial also we shall hear the voice of Lollius raised impulsively in my defence; for Aemilianus is deliberately accusing a man whom he knows to be innocent, a course which comes the more easy to him, since, as I have told you, he has already been convicted of lying in a most important case, heard before the Prefect of the city. Just as a good man studiously avoids the repetition of a sin once committed, so men of depraved character repeat their past offence with increased confidence, and, I may add, the more often they do so, the more openly they display their impudence. For honour is like a garment; the older it gets, the more carelessly it is worn. I think it my duty, therefore, in the interest of my own honour, to refute all my opponent's slanders before I come to the actual indictment itself.

For I am pleading not merely my own cause, but that of philosophy as well, philosophy, whose grandeur is such that she resents even the slightest slur cast upon her perfection as though it were the most serious accusation. Knowing this, Aemilianus' advocates, only a short time ago, poured forth with all their usual loquacity a flood of drivelling accusations, many of which were specially invented for the purpose of blackening my character, while the remainder were such general charges as the uninstructed are in the habit of levelling at philosophers. It is true that we may regard these accusations as mere interested vapourings, bought at a price and uttered to prove their shamelessness worthy of its hire.

It is a recognized practice on the part of professional accusers to let out the venom of their tongues to another's hurt; nevertheless, if only in my own interest, I must briefly refute these slanders, lest I, whose most earnest endeavour it is to avoid incurring the slightest spot or blemish to my fair fame, should seem, by passing over some of their more ridiculous charges, to have tacitly admitted their truth, rather than to have treated them with silent contempt. For a man who has any sense of honour or self-respect must needs — such at least is my opinion — feel annoyed when he is thus abused, however falsely. Even those whose conscience reproaches them with some crime, are strongly moved to anger, when men speak ill of them, although they have been accustomed to such ill report ever since they became evildoers. And even though others say naught of their crimes, they are conscious enough that such charges may at any time deservedly be brought against them. It is therefore doubly vexatious to the good and innocent man when charges are undeservedly brought against him which he might with justice bring against others. For his ears are unused and strange to ill report, and he is so accustomed to hear himself praised that insult is more than he can bear.

If, however, I seem to be anxious to rebut charges which are merely frivolous and foolish, the blame must be laid at the door of those, to whom such accusations, in spite of their triviality, can only bring disgrace. I am not to blame. Ridiculous as these charges may be, their refutation cannot but do me honour.

To begin then, only a short while ago, at the commencement of the indictment, you heard them say, 'He, whom we accuse in your court, is a philosopher of the most elegant appearance and a master of eloquence not merely in Latin but also in Greek!' What a damning insinuation! Unless I am mistaken, those were the very words with which Tannonius Pudens, whom no one could accuse of being a master of eloquence, began the indictment.

I wish that these serious reproaches of beauty and eloquence had been true. It would have been easy to answer in the words, with which Homer makes Paris reply to Hector which I may interpret thus: 'The most glorious gifts of the gods are in no wise to be despised; but the things which they are wont to give are withheld from many that would gladly possess them.' Such would have been my reply.

I should have added that philosophers are not forbidden to possess a handsome face. Pythagoras, the first to take the name of 'philosopher', was the handsomest man of his day. Zeno also, the ancient philosopher of Velia, who was the first to discover that most ingenious device of refuting hypotheses by the method of self-inconsistency, that same Zeno was — so Plato asserts — by far the most striking in appearance of all the men of his generation. It is further recorded of many other philosophers that they were comely of countenance and added fresh charm to their personal beauty by their beauty of character.

But such a defence is, as I have already said, far from me. Not only has nature given me but a commonplace appearance, but continued literary labour has swept away such charm as my person ever possessed, has reduced me to a lean habit of body, sucked away all the freshness of life, destroyed my complexion and impaired my vigour. As to my hair, which they with unblushing mendacity declare I have allowed to grow long as an enhancement to my personal attractions, you can judge of its elegance and beauty. As you see, it is tangled, twisted and unkempt like a lump of tow, shaggy and irregular in length, so knotted and matted that the tangle is past the art of man to unravel. This is due not to mere carelessness in the tiring of my hair, but to the fact that I never so much as comb or part it. I think this is a sufficient refutation of the accusations concerning my hair which they hurl against me as though it were a capital charge.

As to my eloquence — if only eloquence were mine — it would be small matter either for wonder or envy if I, who from my earliest years to the present moment have devoted myself with all my powers to the sole study of literature and for this spurned all other pleasures, had sought to win eloquence to be mine with toil such as few or none have ever expended, ceasing neither night nor day, to the neglect and impairment of my bodily health. But my opponents need fear nothing from my eloquence. If I have made any real advance therein, it is my aspirations rather than my attainments on which I must base my claim.

Certainly if the aphorism said to occur in the poems of Statius Caecilius be true, that innocence is eloquence itself, to that extent I may lay claim to eloquence and boast that I yield to none. For on that assumption what living man could be more eloquent than myself? I have never even harboured in my thoughts anything to which I should fear to give utterance. Nay, my eloquence is consummate, for I have ever held all sin in abomination; I have the highest oratory at my command, for I have uttered no word, I have done no deed, of which I need fear to discourse in public. I will begin therefore to discourse of those verses of mine, which they have produced as though they were something of which I ought to be ashamed. You must have noticed the laughter with which I showed my annoyance at the absurd and illiterate manner in which they recited them.

They began by reading one of my jeux d'esprit, a brief letter in verse, addressed to a certain Calpurnianus on the subject of a tooth-powder. When Calpurnianus produced my letter as evidence against me, his desire to do me a hurt blinded him to the fact that if anything in the letter could be urged as a reproach against me, he shared in that reproach. For the verses testify to the fact that he had asked me to send him the wherewithal to clean his teeth:

> Good morrow! Friend Calpurnianus, take
> the salutation these swift verses make.
> Wherewith I send, responsive to thy call,
> a powder rare to cleans thy teeth withal.
> This delicate dust of Arab spices fine,
> shall smooth the swollen gums and sweep away
> the relics of the feast of yesterday.
> So shall no foulness, no dark smirch be seen,
> if laughter shown thy teeth their lips between.

I ask you, what is there in these verses that is disgusting in point either of matter or of manner? What is there that a philosopher should be ashamed to own? Unless indeed I am to blame for sending a powder made of Arabian spices to Calpurnianus, for whom it would be more suitable that he should

> Polish his teeth and ruddy gums,

as Catullus says, after the filthy fashion in vogue among the Iberians.

I saw a short while back that some of you could scarcely restrain your laughter, when our orator treated these views of mine on the cleansing of the teeth as a matter for savage denunciation, and condemned my administration of a toothpowder with fiercer indignation than has ever been shown in condemning the administration of a poison.

Of course it is a serious charge, and one that no philosopher can afford to despise, to say of a man that he will not allow a speck of dirt to be seen upon his person, that he will not allow any visible portion of his body to be offensive or unclean, least of all the mouth, the organ used most frequently, openly and conspicuously by man, whether to kiss a friend, to conduct a conversation, to speak in public, or to offer up prayer in some temple. Indeed speech is the prelude to every kind of action and, as the greatest of poets says, proceeds from 'the barrier of our teeth'. If there were any one present here today with like command of the grand style, he might say after his fashion that those above all men who have any care for their manner of speaking, should pay closer attention to their mouth than to any other portion of their body, for it is the soul's antechamber, the portal of speech, and the gathering place where thoughts assemble. I myself should say that in my poor judgement there is nothing less seemly for a freeborn man with the education of a gentleman than an unwashen mouth. For man's mouth is in position exalted, to the eye conspicuous, in use eloquent. True, in wild beasts and cattle the mouth is placed low and looks downward to the feet, is in close proximity to their food and to the path thq tread, and is hardly ever conspicuous save when its owner is dead or infuriated with a desire to bite. But there is no part of man that sooner catches the eye when he is silent, or more often when he speaks.

I should be obliged, therefore, if my critic Aemilianus would answer me and tell me whether he is ever in the habit of washing his feet, or, if he admits that he is in the habit of so doing, whether he is prepared to argue that a man should pay more attention to the cleanliness of his feet than to that of his teeth.

Certainly, if like you, Aemilianus, he never opens his mouth save to utter slander and abuse, I should advise him to pay no attention to the state of his mouth nor to attempt to remove the stains from his teeth with oriental powders: he would be better employed in rubbing them with charcoal from some funeral pyre. Least of all should he wash them with common water; rather let his guilty tongue, the chosen servant of lies and bitter words, rot in the filth and ordure that it loves! Is it reasonable, wretch, that your tongue should be fresh and clean, when your voice is foul and loathsome, or that, like the viper, you should employ snow-white teeth for the emission of dark, deadly poison? On the other hand it is only right that, just as we wash a vessel that is to hold good liquor, he who knows that his words will be at once useful and agreeable should cleanse his mouth as a prelude to speech.

But why should I speak further of man? Even the crocodile, the monster of the Nile — so they tell me — opens his jaws in all innocence, that his teeth may be cleaned. For his mouth being large, tongueless, and continually open in the water, multitudes of leeches become entangled in his teeth: these, when the crocodile emerges from the river and opens his mouth, are removed by a friendly waterbird, which is allowed to insert its beak without any risk to itself.

But enough of this! I now come to certain other of my verses, which according to them are amatory; but so vilely and coarsely did they read them as to leave no impression save one of disgust. Now what has it to do with the malpractices of the black art, if I write poems in praise of the boys of my friend Scribonius Laetus? Does the mere fact of my being a poet make me a wizard? Who ever heard any orator produce such likely ground for suspicion, such apt conjectures, such close-reasoned argument? 'Apuleius has written verses!' If they are bad, that is something against him as a poet, but not as a philosopher. If they are good, why do you accuse him? 'But they were frivolous verses of an erotic character.' So that is the charge you bring against me? and it was a mere slip of the tongue when you indicted me for practising the black art?

And yet many others have written such verse, although you may be ignorant of the fact. Among the Greeks, for instance, there was a certain Teian, there was a Lacedaemonian, a Cean, and countless others; there was even a woman, a Lesbian, who wrote with such grace and such passion that the sweetness of her song makes us forgive the impropriety of her words; among our own poets there were Aedituus, Porcius, and Catulus, with countless others. 'But they were not philosophers.' Will you then deny that Solon was a serious man and a philosopher? Yet he is the author of that most wanton verse:

Longing for your thighs and your sweet mouth.

What is there so lascivious in all my verses compared with that one line? I will say nothing of the writings of Diogenes the Cynic, of Zeno the founder of Stoicism, and many other similar instances. Let me recite my own verses afresh, that my opponents may realize that I am not ashamed of them:

Critias my treasure is and you,
light of my life, Charinus, too
hold in my love-tormented heart
your own inalienable part.
Ah! Doubt not! With redoubled spite
though fire on fire consume me quite,
the flames ye kindle, boys divine,
I can endure, so ye be mine.
Only to each may I be dear
as your own selves are, and as near;
grant only this and you shall be
dear as mine own two eyes to be.

Now let me read you the others also which they read last as being the most intemperate in expression.

I lay these garlands, Critias sweet,
and this my song before thy feet;
song to thyself I dedicate,
wreaths to the Angel of thy fate.
The song I send to hymn the praise
of this, the best of all glad days,

whereon the circling seasons bring
the glory of thy fourteenth spring;
the garlands, that thy brows may shine
with splendour worthy spring's and thine,
that thou in boyhood's golden hours
mayst deck the flower of life with flowers.
Wherefore for these bright blooms of spring
thy springtide sweet surrendering,
the tribute of my love repay
and all my gifts with thine outweigh.
Surpass the twined garland's grace
with arms entwined in soft embrace;
the crimson of the rose eclipse
with kisses from thy rosy lips.
Or if thou wilt, be this my meed
and breathe thy soul into the reeds!
then shall my songs be shamed and mute
before the music of thy flute.

 This, Maximus, is what they throw in my teeth, as though it were the work of an infamous rake: verses about garlands and serenades.

 You must have noticed also that in this connexion they further attack me for calling these boys Charinus and Critias, which are not their true names. On this principle they may as well accuse Caius Catullus for calling Clodia Lesbia, Ticidas for substituting the name Perilla for that of Metella, Propertius for concealing the name Hostia beneath the pseudonym of Cynthia, and Tibullus for singing of Delia in his verse, when it was Plania who ruled his heart. For my part I should rather blame Caius Lucilius, even allowing him all the license of a satiric poet, for prostituting to the public gaze the boys Gentius and Macedo, whose real names he mentions in his verse without any attempt at concealment. How much more reserved is Mantua's poet, who, when like myself he praised the slave-boy of his friend Pollio in one of his light pastoral poems, shrinks from mentioning real nnames and calls himself Corydon and the boy Alexis.

But Aemilianus, whose rusticity far surpasses that of the Virgilean shepherds and cowherds, who is, in fact, and always has been a boor and a barbarian, though he thinks himself far more austere than Serranus, Curius, or Fabricius, those heroes of the days of old, denies that such verses are worthy of a philosopher who is a follower of Plato. Will you persist in this attitude, Aemilianus, if I can show that my verses were modelled upon Plato? For the only verses of Plato now extant are love-elegies, the reason, I imagine, being that he burned all his other poems because they were inferior in charm and finish. Learn then the verses written by Plato in honour of the boy Aster, though I doubt if at your age it is possible for you to become a man of learning.

Thou wert the morning star among the living
ere thy fair light had fled; —
now having died, thou art as Hesperus giving
new light unto the dead.

There is another poem by Plato dealing conjointly with the boys Alexis and Phaedrus:

I lid but breathe the words 'Alexis fair',
and all men gazed on him with wondering eyes,
my soul, why point to questing beasts their prize?
'Twas thus we lost our Phaedrus; ah! Beware!

Without citing any further examples I will conclude by quoting a line addressed by Plato to Dion of Syracuse:

Dion, with love thou hast distraught my soul.

Which of us is most to blame? I who am fool enough to speak seriously of such things in a lawcourt? Or you who are slanderous enough to include such charges in your indictment? For sportive effusions in verse are valueless as evidence of a poet's morals. Have you not read Catullus, who replies thus to those who wish him ill:

A virtuous poet must be chaste. Agreed.
But for his verses there is no such need.

The divine Hadrian, when he honoured the tomb of his friend the poet Voconius with an inscription in verse from his own pen, wrote thus:

Thy verse was wanton, but thy soul was chaste,

words which he would never have written had he regarded verse of somewhat too lively a wit as proving their author to be a man of immoral life. I remember that I have read not a few poems by the divine Hadrian himself which were of the same type. Come now, Aemilianus, I dare you to say that that was ill done which was done by an emperor and censor, the divine Hadrian, and once done was recorded for subsequent generations.

But, apart from that, do you imagine that Maximus will censure anything that has Plato for its model, Plato whose verses, which I have just read, are all the purer for being frank, all the more modest for being outspoken? For in these matters and the like, dissimulation and concealment is the mark of the sinner, open acknowledgement and publication a sign that the writer is but exercising his wit. For nature has bestowed on innocence a voice wherewith to speak, but to guilt she has given silence to veil its sin.

I say nothing of those lofty and divine Platonic doctrina, that are familiar to but few of the elect and wholly unknown to all the uninitiate, such for instance as that which teaches us that Venus is not one goddess, but two, each being strong in her own type of love and several types of lovers. The one is the goddess of the common herd, who is fired by base and vulgar passion and commands not only the hearts of men, but cattle and wild beasts also, to give themselves over to the gratification of their desires: she strikes down these creatures with fierce intolerable force and fetters their servile bodies in the embraces of lust. The other is a celestial power endued with lofty and generous passion: she cares for none save men, and of them but few; she neither stings nor lures her followers to foul deeds. Her love is neither wanton nor voluptuous, but serious and unadorned, and wins her lovers to the pursuit of virtue by revealing to them how fair a thing is nobility of soul. Or, if ever she commends beautiful bodies to their admiration, she puts a bar upon all indecorous conduct. For the only claim that physical beauty has upon the admiration is that it reminds those whose souls have soared above things human to things divine, of that beauty which once they beheld in all its truth and purity enthroned among the gods in heaven. Wherefore let us admit that Afranius shows his usual beauty of expression when he says: 'Only the sage can love, only desire is known to others'; although if you would know the real truth, Aemilianus, or if you are capable of ever comprehending such high matters, the sage does not love, but only remembers.

I would therefore beg you to pardon the philosopher Plato for his amatory verse, and relieve me of the necessity of offending against the precepts put by Ennius into the mouth of Neoptolemus by philosophizing at undue length; on the other hand if you refuse to pardon Plato, I am quite ready to suffer blame on this count in his company.

I must express my deep gratitude to you, Maximus, for listening with such close attention to these side issues, which are necessary to my defence inasmuch as I am paying back my accusers in their own coin. Your kindness emboldens me to make this further request, that you will listen to all that I have to say by way of prelude to my answer to the main charge with the same courtesy and attention that you have hitherto shown.

For next I have to deal with that long oration, austere as any censor's, which Pudens delivered on the subject of my mirror. He nearly exploded, so violently did he declaim against the horrid nature of my offence. 'The philosopher owns a mirror, the philosopher actually possesses a mirror.' Grant that I possess it: if I denied it, you might really think that your accusation had gone home: still it is by no means a necessary inference that I am in the habit of adorning myself before a mirror. Why! suppose I possessed a theatrical wardrobe, would you venture to argue from that that I am in the frequent habit of wearing the trailing robes of tragedy, the saffron cloak of the mimic dance, or the patchwork suit of the harlequinade? I think not. On the contrary there are plenty of things of which I enjoy the use without the possession.

But if possession is no proof of use nor non-possession of non-use, and if you complain of the fact that I look into the mirror rather than that I possess it, you must go on to show when and in whose presence I have ever looked into it; for as things stand, you make it a greater crime for a philosopher to look upon a mirror than for the uninitiated to gaze upon the mystic emblems of Ceres.

Come now, let me admit that I have looked into it. Is it a crime to be acquainted with one's own likeness and to carry it with one wherever one goes ready to hand within the compass of a small mirror, instead of keeping it hidden away in some one place? Are you ignorant of the fact that there is nothing more pleasing for a man to look upon than his own image? At any rate I know that fathers love those sons most who most resemble themselves, and that public statues are decreed as a reward for merit that the original may gladden his heart by looking on them. What else is the significance of statues and portraits produced by the various arts? You will scarcely maintain the paradox that what is worthy of admiration when produced by art is blameworthy when produced by nature; for nature has an even greater facility and truth than art.

Long labour is expended over all the portraits wrought by the hand of man, yet they never attain to such truth as is revealed by a mirror. Clay is lacking in life, marble in colour, painting in solidity, and all three in motion, which is the most convincing element in a likeness: whereas in a mirror the reflection of the image is marvellous, for it is not only like its original, but moves and follows every nod of the man to whom it belongs; its age always corresponds to that of those who look into the mirror, from their earliest childhood to their expiring age: it puts on all the changes brought by the advance of years, shares all the varying habits of the body, and imitates the shifting expressions of joy and sorrow that may be seen on the face of one and the same man. For all we mould in clay or cast in bronze or carve in stone or tint with encaustic pigments or colour with paint, in a word, every attempt at artistic representation by the hand of man after a brief lapse of time loses in truth and becomes motionless and impassive like the face of a corpse. So far superior to all pictorial art in respect of truthful representation is that craftsmanly smoothness and productive splendour of the mirror.

Two alternatives then are before us. We must either follow the precept of the Lacedaemonian Agesilaus, who had no confidence in his personal appeannce and refused to allow his portrait to be painted or carved; or we must accept the universal custom of the rest of mankind which welcomes portraiture both in sculpture and painting. In the latter case, is there any reason for preferring to see one's portrait moulded in marble rather than reflected in silver, in a painting rather than in a mirror?

Or do you regard it as disgraceful to pay continual attention to one's own appearance? Is not Socrates said actually to have urged his followers frequently to consider their image in a glass, that so those of them that prided themselves on their appearance might above all else take care that they did no dishonour to the splendour of their body by the blackness of their hearts; while those who regarded themselves as less than handsome in personal appearance might take especial pains to conceal the meanness of their body by the glory of their virtue? You see; the wisest man of his day actually went so far as to use the mirror as an instrument of moral discipline. Again, who is ignorant of the fact that Demosthenes, the greatest master of the art of speaking, always practised pleading before a mirror as though before a professor of rhetoric? When that supreme orator had drained deep draughts of eloquence in the study of Plato the philosopher, and had learned all that could be learned of argumentation from the dialectician Eubulides, last of all he betook himself to a mirror to learn perfection of delivery. Which do you think should pay greatest attention to the decorousness of his appearance in the delivery of a speech? The orator when he wrangles with his opponent or the philosopher when he rebukes the vices of mankind? The man who harangues for a brief space before an audience of jurymen drawn by the chance of the lot, or he who is continually discoursing with all mankind for audience? The man who is quarrelling over the boundaries of lands, or he whose theme is the boundaries of good and evil?

Moreover there are other reasons why a philosopher should look into a mirror. He is not always concerned with the contemplation of his own likeness, he contemplates also the causes which produce that likeness. Is Epicurus right when he asserts that images proceed forth from us, as it were a kind of slough that continually streams from our bodies? These images when they strike anything smooth and solid are reflected by the shock and reversed in such wise as to give back an image turned to face its original. Or should we accept the view maintained by other philosophers that rays are emitted from our body? According to Plato these rays are filtered forth from the centre of our eyes and mingle and blend with the light of the world without us; according to Archytas they issue forth from us without any external support; according to the Stoics these rays are called into action by the tension of the air: all agree that, when these emanations strike any dense, smooth, and shining surface, they return to the surface from which they proceeded in such manner that the angle of incidence is equal to the angle of reflection, and as a result that which they approach and touch without the mirror is imaged within the mirror.

What do you think? Should not philosophers make all these problems subjects of research and inquiry and in solitary study look into mirrors of every kind, liquid and solid? There is also over and above these questions further matter for discussion. For instance, why is it that in flat mirrors all images and objects reflected are shown in almost precisely their original dimensions, whereas in convex and spherical mirrors everything is seen smaller, in concave mirrors on the other hand larger than nature? Why again and under what circumstances are left and right reversed? When does one and the same mirror seem now to withdraw the image into its depths, now to extrude it forth to view? Why do concave mirrors when held at right angles to the rays of the sun kindle tinder set opposite them? What is the cause of the prismatic colours of the rainbow, or of the appearance in heaven of two rival images of the sun, with sundry other phenomena treated in a monumental volume by Archimedes of Syracuse, a man who showed extraordinary and unique subtlety in all branches of geometry, but was perhaps particularly remarkable for his frequent and attentive inspection of mirrors.

If you had only read this book, Aemilianus, and, instead of devoting yourself to the study of your fields and their dull clods, had studied the mathematician's slate and blackboard, believe me, although your face is hideous enough for a tragic mask of Thyestes, you would assuredly, in your desire for the acquisition of knowledge, look into the glass and sometimes leave your plough to marvel at the numberless furrows with which wrinkles have scored your face.

But I should not be surprised if you prefer me to speak of your ugly deformity of a face and to be silent about your morals, which are infinitely more repulsive than your features. I will say nothing of them. In the first place I am not naturally of a quarrelsome disposition, and secondly I am glad to say that until quite recently you might have been white or black for all I knew. Even now my knowledge of you is inadequate. The reason for this is that your rustic occupations have kept you in obscurity, while I have been occupied by my studies, and so the shadow cast about you by your insignificance has shielded your character from scrutiny, while I for my part take no interest in others' ill deeds, but have always thought it more important to conceal my own faults than to track out those of others. As a result you have the advantage of one who, while he is himself shrouded in darkness, surveys another who chances to have taken his stand in the full light of day. You from your darkness can with ease form an opinion as to what I am doing in my not undistinguished position before all the world; but your position is so abject, so obscure, and so withdrawn from the light of publicity that you are by no means so conspicuous.

I neither know nor care to know whether you have slaves to till your fields or whether you do so by interchange of service with your neighbours. But you know that at Oea I gave three slaves their freedom on the same day, and your advocate has cast it in my teeth together with other actions of mine of which you have given him information. And yet but a few minutes earlier he had declared that I came to Oea accompanied by no more than one slave. I challenge you to tell me how I could have made one slave into three free men. But perhaps this is one of my feats of magic. Has lying made you blind, or shall I rather say that from force of habit you are incapable of speaking the truth? 'Apuleius,' you say, 'came to Oea with one slave,' and then only a very few words later you blurt out, 'Apuleius on one and the same day at Oea gave three slaves their freedom.' Not even the assertion that I had come with three slaves and had given them all their freedom would have been credible: but suppose I had done so, what reason do you have for regarding three slaves as a mark of my poverty, rather than for considering three freed men as a proof of my wealth?

You don't know, really, Aemilianus, you don't know how to accuse a philosopher: you reproach me for the scantiness of my household, whereas it would really have been my duty to have laid claim, however falsely, to such poverty. It would have redounded to my credit, for I know that not only philosophers of whom I boast myself a follower, but also generals of the Roman people have gloried in the small number of their slaves. Have your advocates really never read that Marcus Antonius, a man who had filled the office of consul, had but eight slaves in his house? That that very Carbo who obtained supreme control of Rome had fewer by one? That Manius Curius, famous beyond all men for the crowns of victory that he had won, Manius Curius who thrice led the triumphal procession through the same gate of Rome, had but two servants to attend him in camp, so that in good truth that same man who triumphed over the Sabines, the Samnites, and Pyrrhus had fewer slaves than triumphs? Marcus Cato did not wait for others to tell it of him, but himself records the fact in one of his speeches that when he set out as consul for Spain he took but three slaves from the city with him. When, however, he came to stay at a state residence, the number seemed insufficient, and he ordered two slaves to be bought in the market to wait on him at table, so that he took five in all to Spain.

Had Pudens come across these facts in his reading, he would, I think, either have omitted this particular slander or would have preferred to reproach me on the ground that three slaves were too large rather than too small an establishment for a philosopher.

Pudens actually reproached me with being poor, a charge which is welcome to a philosopher and one that he may glory in. For poverty has long been the handmaid of philosophy; frugal and sober, she is content with little, greedy for naught save honour, a stable possession in the face of wealth, her mien is free from care, and her adornment simple; her counsels are beneficent, she puffs no man up with pride, she corrupts no man with passions beyond his control, she maddens no man with the lust for power, she neither desires nor can indulge in the pleasures of feasting and of sex. These sins and their like are usually the nurslings of wealth. Count over all the greatest crimes recorded in the history of mankind, you will find no poor man among their guilty authors. On the other hand, it is rare to find wealthy men among the great figures of history. All those at whom we marvel for their great deeds were the nurslings of poverty from their very cradles, poverty that founded all cities in the days of old, poverty mother of all arts, witless of all sin, bestower of all glory, crowned with all honour among all the peoples of the world. Take the history of Greece: the justice of poverty is seen in Aristides, her benignity in Phocion, her force in Epaminondas, her wisdom in Socrates, her eloquence in Homer. It was this same poverty that established the empire of the Roman people in its first beginnings, and even to this day Rome offers up thanksgivings for it to the immortal gods with libations poured from a wooden ladle and offerings borne in an earthen platter. If the judges sitting to try this case were Caius Fabricius, Gnaeus Scipio, Manius Curius, whose daughters on account of their poverty were given dowries from the public treasury and so went to their husbands bringing with them the honour of their houses and the wealth of the state; if Publicola, who drove out the Kings, or Agrippa, the healer of the people's strife, men whose funerals were on account of their poverty enriched by the gift of a few farthings per man from the whole Roman people; if Atilius Regulus, whose lands on account of his own poverty were cultivated at the public expense; if, in a word, all the heroes of the old Roman stock, consuls and censors and triumphant generals, were given a brief renewal of life and sent back to earth to give hearing to this case, would you dare in the presence of so many poor consuls to reproach a philosopher with poverty?

Perhaps Claudius Maximus seems to you to be a suitable person before whom to deride poverty, because he himself is in enjoyment of great wealth and enormous opulence? You are wrong, Aemilianus, you are wholly mistaken in your estimate of his character, if you take the bounty of his fortune rather than the sternness of his philosophy as the standard for your judgement and fail to realize that one, who holds so austere a creed and has so long endured military service, is more likely to befriend a moderate fortune with all its limitations than opulence with all its luxury, and holds that fortunes, like tunics, should be comfortable, not long. For even a Fortune, if cannot be carried but must be dragged, will entangle and trip the feet as badly as a cloak that hangs down in front. In everything that we employ for the needs of daily life, whatever exceeds the mean is superfluous and a burden rather than a help. So it is that excessive riches, like steering oars of too great weight and bulk, serve to sink the ship rather than to guide it; for their bulk is unprofitable and their superfluity a curse.

I have noticed that of the wealthy themselves those win most praise who live quietly and in moderate comfort, concealing their actual resources, administering their great possessions without ostentation or pride and showing like poor folk under the disguise of their moderation. Now, if even the rich to some extent affect the outward form and semblance of poverty to give evidence of their moderation, why should we of slenderer means be ashamed of being poor not in appearance only but in reality?

I might even engage with you in controversy over the word poverty, urging that no man is poor who rejects the superfluous and has at his command all the necessities of life, which nature has ordained should be exceedingly small. For he who desires least will possess most, inasmuch as he who wants but little will have all he wants. The measure of wealth ought therefore not to be the possession of lands and investments, but the very soul of man. For if avarice make him continually in need of some fresh acquisition and insatiable in his lust for gain, not even mountains of gold will bring him satisfaction, but he will always be begging for more that he may increase what he already possesses. That is the genuine admission of poverty. For every desire for fresh acquisition springs from the consciousness of want, and it matters little how large your possessions are if they are too small for you. Philus had a far smaller household than Laelius, Laelius than Scipio, Scipio than Crassus the Rich, and yet not even Crassus had as much as he wanted; and so, though he surpassed all others in wealth, he was himself surpassed by his own avarice and seemed rich to all save himself. On the other hand, the philosophers of whom I have spoken wanted nothing beyond what was at their disposal, and, thanks to the harmong existing between their desires and their resources, they were deservedly rich and happy. For poverty consists in the need for fresh acquisition, wealth in the satisfaction springing from the absence of needs. For the badge of penury is desire, the badge of wealth contempt.

Therefore, Aemilianus, if you wish me to be regarded as poor, you must first prove that I am avaricious. But if my soul lacks nothing, I care little how much of the goods of this world be lacking to me; for it is no honour to possess them and no reproach to lack them.

But let us suppose it to be otherwise. Suppose that I am poor, because fortune has grudged me riches, because my guardian, as often happens, misappropriated my inheritance, some enemy robbed me, or my father left me nothing. Is it just to reproach a man for that which is regarded as no reproach to the animal kingdom, to the eagle, to the bull, to the lion? If the horse is strong in the possession of his peculiar excellences, if he is pleasant to ride and swift in his paces, no one rebukes him for the poverty of his food. Must you then reproach me, not for any scandalous word or deed, but simply because I live in a small house, possess an unusually small number of slaves, subsist on unusually light diet, wear unusually light clothing, and make unusually small purchaches of food?

Yet however scanty my service, food, and raiment may seem to you, I on the contrary regard them as ample and even excessive. Indeed I am desirous of still further reducing them, since the leas I have to distract me the happier I shall be. For the soul, like the body, goes lightly clad when in good health; weakness wraps itself up, and it is a sure sign of infirmity to have many wants. We live, just as we swim, all the better for being but lightly burdened. For in this stormy life as on the stormy ocean heavy things sink us and light things buoy us up. It is in this respect, I find, that the gods more especially surpass men, namely that they lack nothing: wherefore he of mankind whose needs are smallest is most like unto the gods.

I therefore regarded it as a compliment when to insult me you asserted that my whole household consisted of a wallet and a staff. Would that my spirit were made of such stern stuff as to permit me to dispense with all this furniture and worthily to carry that equipment for which Crates sacrificed all his wealth! Crates, I tell you, though I doubt if you will believe me, Aemilianus, was a man of great wealth and honour among the nobility of Thebes; but for love of this habit, which you cast in my face as a crime, he gave his large and luxurious household to his fellow citizens, resigned his troops of slaves for solitude, so contemned the countless trees of his rich orchards as to be content with one staff, exchanged his elegant villas for one small wallet, which, when he had fully appreciated its utility, he even praised in song by diverting from their original meaning certain lines of Homer in which he extols the island of Crete. I will quote the first lines, that you may not think this a mere invention of mine designed to meet the needs of my own case:

There is a twon named Wallet in the midst
of smoke that's dark as wine.

The lines which follow are so wonderful, that had you read them you would envy me my wallet even more than you envy me my marriage with Pudentilla.

You reproach philosophers for their staff and wallet. You might as well reproach cavalry for their trappings, infantry for their shields, standard-bearers for their banners, triumphant generals for their chariots drawn by four white horses and their cloaks embroidered with palmleaves. The staff and wallet are not, it is true, carried by the Platonic philosophers, but are the badges of the Cynic school. To Diogenes and Antisthenes they were what the crown is to the king, the cloak of purple to the general, the cowl to the priest, the trumpet to the augur. Indeed the Cynic Diogenes, when he disputed with Alexander the Great, as to which of the two was the true king, boasted of his staff as the true sceptre. The unconquered Hercules himself, since you despise my instances as drawn from mere mendicancy, Hercules that roamed the whole world, exterminated monsters, and conquered races, god though he was, had but a skin for raiment and a staff for company in the days when he wandered through the earth. And yet but a brief while afterwards he was admitted to heaven as a reward for his virtue.

But if you despise these examples and challenge me, not to plead my case, but to enter into a discussion of the amount of my fortune, to put an end to your ignorance on this point, if it exists, I acknowledge that my father left my brother and myself a little under 2,000,000 sesterces — a sum on which my lengthy travels, continual studies, and frequent generosity have made considerable inroads. For I have often assisted my friends and have shown substantial gratitude to many of my instructors, on more than one occasion going so far as to provide dowries for their daughters. Nay, I should not have hesitated to expend every farthing of my patrimony, if so I might acquire what is far better by contempt for my patrimony. But as for you, Aemilianus, and ignorant boors of your kidney, in your case the fortune makes the man. You are like barren and blasted trees that produce no fruit, but are valued only for the timber that their trunks contain.

But I beg you, Aemilianus, in future to abstain from reviling any one for their poverty, since you yourself used, after waiting for some seasonable shower to soften the ground, to expend three days in ploughing single-handed, with the aid of one wretched ass, that miserable farm at Zarath, which was all your father left you. It is only recently that fortune has smiled on you in the shape of wholly undeserved inheritances which have fallen to you by the frequent deaths of relatives, deaths to which, far more than to your hideous face, you owe your nickname of Charon.

As to my birthplace, you assert that my writings prove it to lie right on the marches of Numidia and Gaetulia, for I publicly described myself as half Numidian, half Gaetulian in a discourse delivered in the presence of that most distinguished citizen Lollianus Avitus. I do not see that I have any more reason to be ashamed of that than had the elder Cyrus for being of mixed descent, half Mede, half Persian. A man's birthplace is of no importance, it is his character that matters. We must consider not in what part of the world, but with what purpose he set out to live his life. Sellers of wine and cabbages are permitted to enhance the value of their wares by advertising the excellence of the soil whence they spring, as for instance with the wine of Thasos and the cabbages of Phlius. For those products of the soil are wonderfully improved in flavour by the fertility of the district which produces them, the moistness of the climate, the mildness of the winds, the warmth of the sun, and the richness of the soil. But in the case of man, the soul enters the tenement of the body from without. What, then, can such circumstances as these add to or take away from his virtues or his vices? Has there ever been a time or place in which a race has not produced a variety of intellects, although some races seem stupider and some wiser than others? The Scythians are the stupidest of men, and yet the wise

Anacharsis was a Scyth. The Athenians are shrewd, and yet the Athenian Meletides was a fool.

I say this not because I am ashamed of my country, since even in the time of Syphax we were a township. When he was conquered we were transferred by the gift of the Roman people to the dominion of King Masinissa, and finally as the result of a settlement of veteran soldiers, our second founders, we have become a colony of the highest distinction. In this same colony my father attained to the post of duumvir and became the foremost citizen of the place, after filling all the municipal offices of honour. I myself, immediately after my first entry into the municipal senate, succeeded to my father's position in the community, and, as I hope, am in no ways a degenerate successor, but receive like honour and esteem for my maintenance of the dignity of my position. Why do I mention this? That you, Aemilianus, may be less angry with me in future and may more readily pardon me for having been negligent enough not to select your 'Attic' Zarath for my birthplace.

Are you not ashamed to produce such accusations with such violence before such a judge, to bring forward frivolous and self-contradictory accusations, and then in the same breath to blame me on both charges at once? Is it not a sheer contradiction to object to my wallet and staff on the ground of austerity, to my poems and mirror on the ground of undue levity; to accuse me of parsimony for having only one slave, and of extravagance in having three; to denounce me for my Greek eloquence and my barbarian birth? Awake from your slumber and remember that you are speaking before Claudius Maximus, a man of stern character, burdened with the business of the whole province. Cease, I say, to bring forward these empty slanders. Prove your indictment, prove that I am guilty of ghastly crimes, detestable sorceries, and black art-magic. Why is it that the strength of your speech lies in mere noise, while it is weak and flabby in point of facts?

I will now deal with the actual charge of magic. You spared no violence in fanning the flame of hatred against me. But you have disappointed all men's expectations by your old wives' fables, and the fire kindled by your accusations has burned itself away. I ask you, Maximus, have you ever seen fire spring up among the stubble, crackling sharply, blazing wide and spreading fast, but soon exhausting its flimsy fuel, dying fast away, leaving not a wrack behind? So they have kindled their accusation with abuse and fanned it with words, but it lacks the fuel of facts and, your verdict once given, is destined to leave not a wrack of calumny behind. The whole of Aemilianus' calumnious accusation was centred in the charge of magic. I should therefore like to ask his most learned advocates how, precisely, they would define a magician.

If what I read in a large number of authors is true, namely, that magician is the Persian word for priest, what is there criminal in being a priest and having due knowledge, science, and skill in all ceremonial law, sacrificial duties, and the binding rules of religion, at least if magic consists in that which Plato sets forth in his description of the methods employed by the Persians in the education of their young princes? I remember the very words of that divine philosopher. Let me recall them to your memory, Maximus:

When the boy has reached the age of fourteen he is handed over to the care of men known as the Royal Masters. They are four in number, and are chosen as being the best of the elders of Persia, one the wisest, another the justest, a third the most temperate, a fourth the bravest. And one of these teaches the boy the magic of Zoroaster the son of Oromazes; and this magic is no other than the worship of the gods. He also teaches him the arts of kingship.

Do you hear, you who so rashly accuse the art of magic? It is an art acceptable to the immortal gods, full of all knowledge of worship and of prayer, full of piety and wisdom in things divine, full of honour and glory since the day when Zoroaster and Oromazes established it, high-priestess of the powers of heaven. Nay, it is one of the first elements of princely instruction, nor do they lightly admit any chance person to be a magician, any more than they would admit him to be a king. Plato — if I may quote him again — in another passage dealing with a certain Zalmoxis, a Thracian and also a master of this art has written that magical charms are merely beautiful words. If that is so, why should I be forbidden to learn the fair words of Zalmoxis or the priestly lore. of Zoroaster?

But if these accusers of mine, after the fashion of the common herd, define a magician as one who by communion of speech with the immortal gods has power to do all the marvels that he will, through a strange power of incantation, I really wonder that they are not afraid to attack one whom they acknowledge to be so powerful. For it is impossible to guard against such a mysterious and divine power. Against other dangers we may take adequate precautions. He who summons a murderer before the judge comes into court with an escort of friends; he who denounces a poisoner is unusually careful as to what he eats; he who accuses a thief sets a guard over his possessions. But for the man who exposes a magician, credited with such awful powers, to the danger of a capital sentence, how can escort or precaution or watchmen save him from unforeseen and inevitable disaster? Nothing can save him, and therefore the man who believes in the truth of such a charge as this is certainly the last person in the world who should bring such an accusation.

But it is a common and general error of the uninitiated to bring the following accusations against philosophers. Some of them think that those who explore the origins and elements of material things are irreligious, and assert that they deny the existence of the gods. Take, for instance, the cases of Anaxagoras, Leucippus, Democritus, and Epicurus, and other natural philosophers. Others call those magicians who bestow unusual care on the investigation of the workings of providence and unusual devotion on their worship of the gods, as though, forsooth, they knew how to perform everything that they know actually to be performed. So Epimenides, Orpheus, Pythagoras, and Ostanes were regarded as magicians, while a similar suspicion attached to the 'purifications' of Empedocles, the 'demon' of

Socrates and the 'good' of Plato. I congratulate myself therefore on being admitted to such distinguished company.

I fear, however, Maximus, that you may regard the empty, ridiculous and childish fictions which my opponents have advanced in support of their case as serious charges merely because they have been put forward. 'Why,' says my accuser, 'have you sought out particular kinds of fish?' Why should not a philosopher be permitted to do for the satisfaction of his desire for knowledge what the gourmand is permitted to do for the satisfaction of his gluttony? 'What,' he asks, 'induced a free woman to marry you after thirteen years of widowhood?' As if it were not more remarkable that she should have remained a widow so long. 'Why, before she married you, did she express certain opinions in a letter?' As if anyone should give the reasons for another person's private opinions. 'But,' he goes on, 'although she was your senior in years, she did not despise your youth.' Surely this simply serves to show that there was no need of magic to induce a woman to marry a man, or a widow to wed a bachelor some years her junior. There are more charges equally frivolous. 'Apuleius,' he persists, 'keeps a mysterious object in his house which he worships with veneration.' As if it were not a worse offence to have nothing to worship at all. 'A boy fell to the ground in Apuleius' presence.' What if a young man or even an old man had fallen in my presence through a sudden stroke of disease or merely owing to the slipperiness of the ground? Do you really think to prove your charge of magic by such arguments as these: the fall of a wretched boy, my marriage to my wife, my purchases of fish?

I should run but small risk if I were to content myself with what I have already said and begin my peroration. But since as a result of the length at which my accusers spoke, the water-clock still allows me plenty of time, let us, if there is no objection, consider the charges in detail. I will deny none of them, be they true or false. I will assume their truth, that this great crowd, which has gathered from all directions to hear this case, may clearly understand not only that no true incrimination can be brought against philosophers, but that not even any false charge can be fabricated against them, which — such is their confidence in their innocence — they will not be prepared to admit and to defend, even though it be in their power to deny it.

I will therefore begin by refuting their arguments, and will prove that they have nothing to do with magic. Next I will show that even on the assumption of my being the most consummate magician, I have never given cause or occasion for conviction of any evil practice. I will also deal with the lies with which they have endeavoured to arouse hostility against me, with their misquotation and misinterpretation of my wife's letters, and with my marriage with Pudentilla, whom, as I will proceed to prove, I married for love and not for money. This marriage of ours caused frightful annoyance and distress to Aemilianus. Hence springs all the anger, frenzy, and raving madness that he has shown in the conduct of this accusation.

If I succeed in making all these points abundantly clear and obvious, I shall then appeal to you, Claudius Maximus, and to all here present to bear me out, that the boy Sicinius Pudens, my step-son, through whom and with whose consent his uncle now accuses me, was quite recently stolen from my charge after the death of Pontianus his brother, who was as much his superior in character as in years, and that he was fiercely embittered against myself and his mother through no fault of mine: that he abandoned his study of the liberal arts and cast off all restraint, and — thanks to the education afforded him by this villanous accusation — is more likely to resemble his uncle Aemilianus than his brother Pontianus.

I will now, as I promised, take Aemilianus' ravings one by one, beginning with that charge which you must have noticed was given the place of honour in the accuser's speech, as his most effective method of exciting suspicion against me as a sorcerer, the charge that I had sought to purchase certain kinds of fish from some fishermen. Which of these two points is of the slightest value as affording suspicion of sorcery? That fishermen sought to procure me the fish? Would you have me entrust such a task to gold-embroiderers or carpenters, and, to avoid your calumnies, make them change their trades so that the carpenter would net me the fish, and the fisherman take his place and hew his timber? Or did you infer that the fish were wanted for evil purposes because I paid to get them? I presume, if I had wanted them for a dinner-party, I should have got them for nothing. Why do not you go farther and accuse me on many similar grounds ? I have often bought wine and vegetables, fruit and bread. The principles laid down by you would involve the starvation of all purveyors of dainties. Who will ever venture to purchase food from them, if it be decided that all provisions for which money is given are wanted not for food but for sorcery?

But if there is nothing in all this that can give rise to suspicion, neither the payment of the fishermen to ply their usual trade, to wit, the capture of fish — I may point out that the prosecution never produced any of these fishermen, who are, as a matter of fact, wholly creatures of their imagination — nor the purchase of a common article of sale — the prosecution have never stated the amount paid, for fear that if they mentioned a small sum, it would be regarded as trivial, or if they mentioned a large sum it would fail to win belief, — if, I say, there is no cause for suspicion on any of these grounds, I would ask Aemilianus to tell me what, failing these, induced them to accuse me of magic.

'You seek to purchase fish,' he says. I will not deny it. But, I ask you, is any one who does that a magician? No more, in my opinion, than if I should seek to purchase hares or boar's flesh or fatted capons. Or is there something mysterious in fish and fish alone, hidden from all save sorcerers only? If you know what it is, clearly you are a magician. If you do not know, you must confess that you are bringing an accusation of the nature of which you are entirely ignorant. To think that you should be so ignorant not only of all literature, but even of popular tales, that you cannot even invent charges that will have some show of plausibility! For of what use for the kindling of love is an unfeeling chilly creature like a fish, or indeed anything else drawn from the sea, unless indeed you propose to bring forward in support of your lie the legend that Venus was born from the sea?

I beg you to listen to me, Tannonius Pudens, that you may learn the extent of the ignorance which you have shown by accepting the possession of a fish as a proof of sorcery. If you had read your Vergil, you would certainly have known that very different things are sought for this purpose. He, as far as I recollect, mentions soft garlands and rich herbs and male incense and threads of diverse hues, and, in addition to these, brittle laurel, clay to be hardened, and wax to be melted in the fire. There are also the objects mentioned by him in a more serious poem.

Rank herbs are sought, with milky venom dark
by brazen sickles under moonlight mown;
sought also is that wondrous talisman,
torn from the forehead of the foal at birth
ere yet its dame could snatch it.

But you who take such exception to fish attribute far different instruments to magicians, charms not to be torn from new-born foreheads, but to be cut from scaly backs; not to be plucked from the fields of earth, but to be drawn up from the deep fields of ocean; not to be mowed with sickles, but to be caught on hooks. Finally, when he is speaking of the black art, Vergil mentions poison, you produce an entree; he mentions herbs and young shoots, you talk of scales and bones; he crops the meadow, you search the waves.

I would also have quoted for your benefit similar passages from Theocritus with many others from Homer and Orpheus, from the comic and tragic poets and from the historians, had I not noticed ere now that you were unable to read Pudentilla's letter which was written in Greek. I will, therefore, do no more than cite one Latin poet. Those who have read Laevius will recognize the lines.

Love-charms the warlocks seek through all the world:
The 'lover's knot' they try, the magic wheel,
ribbons and nails and roots and herbs and shoots,

the two-tailed lizard that draws on to love,
and eke the charm that godes the whinnying mare.

You would have made out a far more plausible case by pretending that I made use of such things instead of fish, if only you had possessed the slightest erudition. For the belief in the use of these things is so widespread that you might have been believed. But of what use are fish save to be cooked and eaten at meals? In magic they seem to me to be absolutely useless. I will tell you why I think so.

Many hold Pythagoras to have been a pupil of Zoroaster, and, like him, to have been skilled in magic. And yet it is recorded that once near Metapontum, on the shores of Italy, his home, which his influence had converted into a second Greece, he noticed certain fishermen draw up their net. He offered to buy whatever it might contain, and after depositing the price ordered all the fish caught in meshes of the net to be relea~ed and thrown back into the sea. He would assuredly never have allowed them to slip from his possession had he known them to possess any valuable magical properties. For being a man of abnormal learning, and a great admirer of the men of old, he remembered that Homer, a poet of manifold or, rather I should say, absolute knowledge of all that may be known, spoke of the power of all the drugs that earth produces, but made no mention of the sea, when speasing of a certain witch, he wrote the line:

All drugs, that wide earth nourishes, she knew.

Similarly in another passage he says:

Earth the grain-giver
yields up to her its store of drugs, whereo
many be healing, mingled in the cup,
and many baneful.

But never in the works of Homer did Proteus anoint his face nor Ulysses his magic trench, nor Aeolus his windbags, nor Helen her mixing bowl, nor Circe her cup, nor Venus her girdle, with any charm drawn from the sea or its inhabitants. You alone within the memory of man have been found to sweep as it were by some convulsion of nature all the powers of herbs and roots and young shoots and small pebbles from their hilltops into the sea, and there confine them in the entrails of fish. And so whereas sorcerers at their rites used to call on Mercury the giver of oracles, Venus that lures the soul, the moon that knows the mystery of the night, and Trivia the mistress of the shades, you will transfer Neptune, with Salacia and Portumnus and all the company of Nereids from the cold tides of the sea to the burning tides of love.

 I have given my reasons for refusing to believe that magicians and fish have anything to do with one another. But now, if it please you, we will assume with Aemilianus that fish are useful for making magical charms as well as for their usual purposes. But does that prove that whoever acquires fish is ipso facto a magician? On those lines it might be urged that whoever acquires a sloop is a pirate, whoever acquires a crowbar a burglar, whoever acquires a sword an assassin. You will say that there is nothing in the world, however harmless, that may not be put to some bad use, nothing so cheerful that it may not be given a gloomy meaning. And yet we do not on that account put a bad interpretation on everything, though, for instance, you should hold that incense, cassia, myrrh, and similar other scents are purchased solely for the purpose of funerals; whereas they are also used for sacrifice and medicine.

 But on the lines of your argument you must believe that even the comrades of Menelaus were magicians; for they, according to the great poet, averted starvation at the isle of Pharos by their use of curved fish-hooks. Nay, you will class in the same category of sorcerers seamews, dolphins, and the lobster; gourmands also, who sink whole fortunes in the sums they pay to fishermen; and fishermen themselves, who by their art capture all manner of fish.

 'But what do you want fish for?' you insist. I feel myself under no necessity to tell you, and refuse to do so. But I challenge you to prove unsupported that I bought them for the purpose you assert; as though I had bought hellebore or hemlock or opium or any other of those drugs, the moderate use of which is salutary, although they are deadly when given with other substances or in too large quantities. Who would endure it if you made this a ground for accusing me of being a poisoner, merely because those drugs are capable of killing a man?

However, let us see what these fish were, fish so necessary for my possession and so hard to find, that they were well worth the price I paid for their acquisition. They have mentioned no more than three. To one they gave a false name; as regards the other two they lied. The name was false, for they asserted that the fish was a sea-hare, whereas it was quite another fish, which Themison, my servant, who knows something of medicine as you heard from his own lips, bought of his own suggestion for me to inspect. For, as a matter of fact, he has not as yet ever come across a sea-hare. But I admit that I search for other kinds of fish as well, and have commissioned not only fishermen but private friends to search for all the rarest kinds of fish, begging them either to describe the appearance of the fish or to send it me, if possible, alive, or, failing that, dead. Why I do so I will soon make clear.

My accusers lied — and very cunning they thought themselves — when they closed their false accusation by pretending that I had sought for two sea-beasts known by gross names. That fellow Tannonius wished to indicate the nature of the obscenity, but failed, matchless pleader that he is, owing to his inability to speak. After long hesitation he indicated the name of one of them by means of some clumsy and disgusting circumlocution. The other he found impossible to describe with decency, and evaded the difficulty by turning to my works and quoting a certain passage from them in which I described the attitude of a statue of Venus.

He also with that lofty puritanism which characterizes him, reproached me for not being ashamed to describe foul things in noble language. I might justly retort on him that, though he openly professes the study of eloquence, that stammering voice of his often gives utterance to noble things so basely as to defile them, and that frequently, when what he has to say presents not the slightest difficulty, he begins to stutter or even becomes utterly tongue-tied. Come now! Suppose I had said nothing about the statue of Venus, nor used the phrase which was of such service to you, what words would you have found to frame a charge, which is as suited to your stupidity as to your powers of speech? I ask you, is there anything more idiotic than the inference that, because the names of two things resemble each other, the things themselves are identical?

Or did you think it a particularly clever invention on your part to pretend that I had sought out these two fish for the purpose of using them as magical charms? Remember that it is as absurd an argument to say that these sea-creatures with gross names were sought for gross purposes, as to say that the sea-comb is sought for the adornment of the hair, the fish named sea-hawk to catch birds, the fish named the little boar for the hunting of boars, or the sea-skull to raise the dead. My reply to these lying fabrications, which are as stupid as they are absurd, is that I have never attempted to acquire these playthings of the sea, these tiny trifles of the shore, either gratis or for money.

Further, I reply that you were quite ignorant of the nature of the objects which you pretended that I sought to acquire. For these worthless fish you mention can be found on any shore in heaps and multitudes, and are cast up on dry land by the merest ripple without any need for human agency. Why do you not say that at the same time I commissioned large numbers of fishermen to secure for me at a price striped sea-shells, rough shells, smooth pebbles, crabs' claws, sea-urchins' husks, the tentacles of cuttlefish, shingle, straws, cordage, not to mention worm-eaten oyster-shells, moss, and seaweed, and all the flotsam of the sea that the winds drive, or the salt wave casts up, or the storm sweeps back, or the calm leaves high and dry all along our shores? For their names are no less suitable than those I mentioned above for the purpose of awakening suspicions.

You have said that certain objects drawn from the sea have a certain value for gross purposes on account of the similarity of their names. On this analogy why should not a stone be good for diseases of the bladder, a shell for the making of a will, a crab for a cancer, seaweed for an ague? Really, Claudius Maximus, in listening to these appallingly long-winded accusations to their very close you have shown a patience that is excessive and a kindness which is too long-suffering. For my part when they uttered these charges of theirs, as though they were serious and cogent, while I laughed at their stupidity, I marvelled at your patience.

However, since he takes so much interest in my affairs, I will now tell Aemilianus why I have examined so many fishes already and why I am unwilling to remain in ignorance of some I have not yet seen. Although he is in the decline of life and suffering from senile decay, let him, if he will, acquire ome learning even at the eleventh hour. Let him read the words of the philosophers of old, that now at any rate he may learn that I am not the first ichthyologist, but follow in the steps of authors, centuries my seniors, such as Aristotle, Theophrastus, Eudemus, Lycon, and the other successors of Plato, who have left many books on the generation, life, parts and differences of animals.

It is a good thing, Maximus, that this case is being tried before a scholar like yourself, who have read Aristotle's numerous volumes 'on the generation, the anatomy, the history of animals', together with his numberless 'Problems' and works by others of his school, treating of various subjects of this kind. If it is an honour and glory to them that they should have put on record the results of their careful researches, why should it be disgraceful to me to attempt the like task, especially since I shall attempt to write on those subjects both in Greek and Latin and in a more concise and systematic manner, and shall strive either to make good omissions or remedy mistakes in all these authors?

I beg of you, if you think it worth while, to permit the reading of extracts from my 'magic' works, that Aemilianus may learn that my sedulous researches and inquiries have a wider range than he thinks. Bring a volume of my Greek works — some of my friends who are interested in questions of natural history may perhaps have them with them in court — take by preference one of those dealing with problems of natural philosophy, and from among those that volume in particular which treats of the race of fish. While he is looking for the book, I will tell you a story which has some relevance to this case.

The poet Sophocles, the rival and survivor of Euripides — for he lived to extreme old age — on being accused by his own son of insanity on the ground that the advance of age had destroyed his wits, is said to have produced that matchless tragedy, his Oedipus Coloneus, on which he happened to be engaged at the time, and to have read it aloud to the jury without adding another word in his defence, except that he bade them without hesitation to condemn him as insane if an old man's poetry displeased them. At that point — so I have read — the jury rose to their feet as one man to show their admiration of so great a poet, and praised him marvellously both for the shrewdness of his argument and for the eloquence of his tragic verse. And indeed they were not far off unanimously condemning the accuser as the madman instead.

Have you found the book? Thank you. Let us try now whether what I write may serve me in good stead in a law-court. Read a few lines at the beginning, then some details concerning the fish. And do you while he reads stop the water-clock.

You hear, Maximus. You have doubtless frequently read the like in the wor}s of ancient philosophers. Remember too that these volumes of mine describe fishes only, distinguishing those that spring from the union of the sexes from those which are spontaneously generated from the mud, discussing how often and at what periods of the year the males and females of each species come together, setting forth the distinction established by nature between those of them who are viviparous and those who are oviparous — for thus I translate the Greek phrases zôiotoka and ôiotoka — together with the causes of this distinction and the organic differences by which it is characterized, in a word — for I would not weary you by discussing all the different methods of generation in animals — treating of the distinguishing marks of species, their various manners of life, the difference of their members and ages, with many other points necessary for the man of science but out of place in a law-court.

I will ask that a few of my Latin writings dealing with the same science may be read, in which you will notice some rare pieces of knowledge and names but little known to the Romans; indeed they have never been produced before today, but yet thanks to my toil and study they have been so translated from the Greek, that in spite of their strangeness they are none the less of Latin mintage. Do you deny this, Aemilianus? If so, let your advocates tell me in what Latin author they have ever before read such words as those which I will cause to be recited to you. I will mention only aquatic animals, nor will I make any reference to other animals save in connexion with the characteristics which distinguish them from aquatic creatures. Listen then to what I say. You will cry out at me saying that I am giving you a list of magic names such as are used in Egyptian or Babylonian rites. Selacheia, malacheia, malakostraka, chondrakantha, ostrakoderma, karcharodonta, amphibia, lepidôta, pholidôta, dermoptera, steganopoda, monèrè, sunagelastika — I might continue the list, but it is not worth wasting time over such trifles, and I need time to deal with other charges. Meanwhile read out my translation into Latin of the few names I have just given you.

What do you think? Is it disgraceful for a philosopher who is no rude and unlearned person of the reckless Cynic type, but who remembers that he is a disciple of Plato, is it disgraceful for such an one to know and care for such learning or to be ignorant and indifferent? To know how far such things reveal the workings of providence, or to swallow all the tales his father and mother told him of the immortal gods?

Quintus Ennius wrote a poem on dainties: he there enumerates countless species of fish, which of course he had carefully studied. I remember a few lines and will recite them:

Clipea's sea-weasels are of all the best,
for 'mice' the place is Aenus; oysters rough
in greatest plenty from Abydos come.
The sea-comb's found at Mitylene and
Ambracian Charadrus, and I praise
Brundisian sargus: take him, if he's big.

> Know that Tarentum's small sea-boar is prime;
> the sword-fish at Surrentum thou shouldst buy;
> Blue fish at Cumae. What! Have I passed by
> Scarus? The brain of Jove is not less sweet.
> You catch them large and good off Nestor's home.
> Have I passed by the black-tail and the 'thrush',
> the sea-merle and the shadow of the sea?
> Best to Corcyra go for cuttle-fish,
> for the acarne and the fat sea-skull
> the purple-fish, the little murex too,
> mice of the sea and the sea-urchin sweet.

He glorified many fish in other verses, stating where each was to be found and whether they were best fried or stewed, and yet he is not blamed for it by the learned. Spare then to blame me, who describe things known to few under elegant and appropriate names both in Greek and Latin.

Enough of this! I call your attention to another point. What if I take such interest and possess such skill in medicine as to search for certain remedies in fish? For assuredly as nature with impartial munificence has distributed and implanted many remedies throughout all other created things, so also similar remedies are to be found in fish. Now, do you think it more the business of a magician than of a doctor, or indeed of a philosopher, to know and seek out remedies? For the philosopher will use them not to win money for his purse, but to give assistance to his fellow men. The doctors of old indeed knew how to cure wounds by magic song, as Homer, the most reliable of all the writers of antiquity, tells us, making the blood of Ulysses to be stayed by a chant as it gushed forth from a wound. Now nothing that is done to save life can be matter for accusation.

'But,' says my adversary, 'for what purpose save evil did you dissect the fish brought you by your servant Themison?' As if I had not told you just now that I write treatises on the organs of all kind of animals, describing the place, number and purpose of their various parts, diligently investigating Aristotle's works on anatomy and adding to them where necessary. I am, therefore, greatly surprised that you are only aware of my having inspected one small fish, although I have actually inspected a very large number under all circumstances wherever I might find them, and have, moreover, made no secret of my researches, but conducted them openly before all the world, so that the merest stranger may, if it please him, stand by and observe me. In this I follow the instruction of my masters, who assert that a free man of free spirit should as far as possible wear his thoughts upon his face. Indeed I actually showed this small fish, which you call a sea-hare, to many who stood by.

I do not yet know what name to call it without closer research, since in spite of its rarity and most remarkable characteristics I do not find it described by any of the ancient philosophers. This fish is, as far as my knowledge extends, unique in one respect, for it contains twelve bones resembling the knuckle-bones of a sucking-pig, linked together like a chain in its belly. Apart from this it is boneless. Had Aristotle known this, Aristotle who records as a most remarkable phenomenon the fact that the fish known as the small sea-ass alone of all fishes has its diminutive heart placed in its stomach, he would assuredly have mentioned the fact.

'You dissected a fish,' he says. Who can call this a crime in a philosopher which would be no crime in a butcher or cook? 'You dissected a fish.' Perhaps you object to the fact that it was raw. You would not regard it as criminal if I had explored its stomach and cut up its delicate liver after it was cooked, as you teach the boy Sicinius Pudens to do with his own fish at meals. And yet it is a greater crime for a philosopher to eat fish than to inspect them. Are augurs to be allowed to explore the livers of victims and may not a philosopher look at them too, a philosopher who knows that he can draw omens from every animal, that he is the high-priest of every god? Do you bring that as a reproach against me which is one of the reasons for the admiration with which Maximus and myself regard Aristotle? Unless you drive his works from the libraries and snatch them from the hands of students you cannot accuse me. But enough! I have said almost more on this subject than I ought.

See, too, how they contradict themselves. They say that I sought my wife in marriage with the help of the black art and charms drawn from the sea at the very time when they acknowledge me to have been in the midmost mountains of Gaetulia, where, I suppose, Deucalion's deluge has made it possible to find fish! I am, however, glad that they do not know that I have read Theophrastus' 'On beasts that bite and sting' and Nicander 'On the bites of wild animals'; otherwise they would have accused me of poisoning as well! As a matter of fact I have acquired a knowledge of these subjects thanks to my reading of Aristotle and my desire to emulate him. I owe something also to the advice of my master Plato, who rays that those who make such investigations as these 'pursue a delightful form of amusement which they will never regret.'

Since I have sufficiently cleared up this business of the fish, listen to another of their inventions equally stupid, but much more extravagant and far more wicked. They themselves knew that their argument about the fish was futile and bound to fail. They realized, moreover, its strange absurdity (for who ever heard of fish being scaled and boned for dark purposes of magic?), they realized that it would be better for their fictions to deal with things of more common report, which have ere now been believed. And so they devised the following fiction which does at least fall within the limits of popular credence and rumour. They asserted that I had taken a boy apart to a secret place with a small altar and a lantern and only a few accomplices as witnesses, and there so bewitched him with a magical incantation that he fell in the very spot where I pronounced the charm, and on being awakened was found to be out of his wits. They did not dare to go any further with the lie. To complete their story they should have added that the boy uttered many prophecies.

For this we know is the prize of magical incantations, namely divination and prophecy. And this miracle in the case of boys is confirmed not only by vulgar opinion but by the authority of learned men. I remember reading various relations of the kind in the philosopher Varro, a writer of the highest learning and erudition, but there was the following story in particular. Inquiry was being made at Tralles by means of magic into the probable issue of the Mithridatic war, and a boy who was gazing at an image of Mercury reflected in a bowl of water foretold the future in a hundred and sixty lines of verse. He records also that Fabius, having lost five hundred denarii, came to consult Nigidius; the latter by means of incantations inspired certain boys so that they were able to indicate to him where a pot containing a certain portion of the money had been hidden in the ground, and how the remainder had been dispersed, one denarius having found its way into the possession of Marcus Cato the philosopher. This coin Cato acknowledged he had received from a certain lackey as a contribution to the treasury of Apollo.

I have read this and the like concerning boys and art-magic in several authors, but I am in doubt whether to admit the truth of such stories or no, although I believe Plato when he asserts that there are certain divine powers holding a position and possessing a character midway between gods and men, and that all divination and the miracles of magicians are controlled by them. Moreover it is my own personal opinion that the human soul, especially when it is young and unsophisticated, may by the allurement of music or the soothing influence of sweet smells be lulled into slumber and banished into oblivion of its surroundings so that, as all consciousness of the body fades from the memory, it returns and is reduced to its primal nature, which is in truth immortal and divine; and thus, as it were in a kind of slumber, it may predict the future.

But howsoever these things may be, if any faith is to be put in them, the prophetic boy must, as far as I can understand, be fair and unblemished in body, shrewd of wit and ready of speech, so that a worthy and fair shrine may be provided for the divine indwelling power (if indeed such a power does enter into the boy's body) or that the boy's mind when wakened may quickly apply itself to its inherent powers of divination, find them ready to its use and reproduce their promptings undulled and unimpaired by any loss of memory. For, as Pythagoras said, not every kind of wood is fit to be carved into the likeness of Mercury.

If that be so, tell me who was that healthy, unblemished, intelligent, handsome boy whom I deemed worthy of initiation into such mysteries by the power of my spells. As a matter of fact, Thallus, whom you nentioned, needs a doctor rather than a magician. For the poor wretch is such a victim to epilepsy that he frequently has fits twice or thrice in one day without the need for any incantations, and exhausts all his limbs with his convulsions. His face is ulcerous, his head bruised in front and behind, his eyes are dull, his nostrils distended, his feet stumbling. He may claim to be the greatest of magicians in whose presence Thallus has remained for any considerable time upon his feet. For he is continually lying down, either a seizure or mere weariness causing him to collapse.

Yet you say that it is my incantations that have overwhelmed him, simply because he has once chanced to have a fit in my presence. Many of his fellow servants, whose appearance as witnesses you have demanded, are present in court. They all can tell you why it is they spit upon Thallus, and why no one ventures to eat from the same dish with him or to drink from the same cup. But why do I speak of these slaves? You yourselves have eyes. Deny then, if you dare, that Thallus used to have fits of epilepsy long before I came to Oea, or that has frequently been shown to doctors. Do his fellow slaves, who are at your service, deny this?

I will confess myself guilty of everything, if he has not long since been sent away into the country, far from the sight of all of them, to a distant farm, for fear he should infect the rest of the household. They cannot deny this to be the fact. For the same reason it is impossible for us to produce him here today. The whole of this accusation has been reckless and sudden, and it was only the day before yesterday that Aemilianus demanded that we should produce fifteen slaves before you. The fourteen living in the town are present today. Thallus only is absent owing to the fact that he has been banished to a place some hundred miles distant. However, we have sent a man to bring him here in a carriage.

I ask you, Maximus, to question these fourteen slaves whom we have produced as to where the boy Thallus is and what is the state of his health; I ask you to question my accuser's slaves. They will not deny that this boy is of revolting appearance, that his body is rotten through and through with disease, that he is liable to fits, and is a barbarian and a clodhopper. This is indeed a handsome boy whom you have selected as one who might fairly be produced at the offering of sacrifice, whom one might touch upon the head and clothe in a fair white cloak in expectation of some prophetic reply from his lips! I only wish he were present. I would have entrusted him to your tender mercies, Aemilianus, and would be ready to hold him myself that you might question him. Here in open court before the judges he would have rolled his wild eyes upon you, he would have foamed at the mouth, spat in your face, drawn in his hands convulsively, shaken his head and fallen at last in a fit into your arms.

Here are fourteen slaves whom you bade me produce in court. Why do you refuse to question them? You want one epileptic boy who, you know as well as I, has long been absent from Oea. What clearer evidence of the falseness of your accusations could be desired? Fourteen slaves are present, as you required; you ignore them. One young boy is absent: you concentrate your attack on him. What is it that you want? Suppose Thallus were present. Do you want to prove that he had a fit in my presence? Why, I myself admit it. You say that this was the result of incantation. I answer that the boy knows nothing about it, and that I can prove that it was not so. Even you will not deny that Thallus was epileptic. Why then attribute his fall to magic rather than disease? Was there anything improbable in his suffering that fate in my presence, which he has often suffered on other occasions in the presence of a number of persons?

Nay, even supposing I had thought it a great achievement to cast an epileptic into a fit, why should I use charms when, as I am told by writers on natural history, the burning of the stone named gagates is an equally sure and easy proof of the disease? For its scent is commonly used as a test of the soundness or infirmity of slaves even in the slave-market. Again, the spinning of a potter's wheel will easily infect a man suffering from this disease with its own giddiness. For the sight of its rotations weakens his already feeble mind, and the potter is far more effective than the magician for casting epileptics into convulsions.

You had no reason for demanding that I should produce these slaves; I have good reason for asking you to name those who witnessed that guilty ritual when I cast the moribund Thallus into one of his fits. The only witness you mention is that worthless boy, Sicinius Pudens, in whose name you accuse me. He says that he was present. His extreme youth is no reason why we should reject his sworn evidence, but the fact that he is one of my accusers does detract from his credibility. It would have been easier for you, Aemilianus, and your evidence would have carried much more weight, had you said that you were present at the rite and had been mad ever since, instead of entrusting the whole business to the evidence of boys as though it were a mere joke. A boy had a fit, a boy saw him. Was it also some boy that bewitched him?

At this point Tannonius Pudens, like the old hand he is, saw that this lie also was falling flat and was doomed to failure by the frowns and murmurs of the audience, and so, in order to check the suspicions of some of them by kindling fresh expectations, he said that he would produce other boys as well whom I had similarly bewitched. He thus passed to another line of accusation.

I might ignore it, but I will go out of my way to challenge it as I have done with all the rest. I want those boys to be produced. I hear they have been bribed by the promise of their liberty to perjure themselves. But I say no more. Only produce them. I demand and insist, Tannonius Pudens, that you should fulfil your promise. Bring forward those boys in whose evidence you put your trust; produce them, name them. You may use the time allotted to my speech for the purpose. Speak, I say, Tannonius.

Why are you silent? Why do you hesitate? Why look round? If he does not remember what he has said, or has forgotten his witnesses' names, do you at any rate, Aemilianus, come forward and tell us what instructions you gave your advocate, and produce those boys. Why do you turn pale? Why are you silent? Is this the way to bring an accusation? Is this the way to indict a man on so serious a charge? Is it not rather an insult to so distinguished a citizen as Claudius Maximus, and a false and slanderous persecution of myself?

However, if your representative has made a slip in his speech, and there are no such boys to produce, at any rate make some use of the fourteen whom I have brought into court. If you refuse, why did you demand the appearance of such a housefull?

You have demanded fifteen slaves to support an accusation of magic; how many would you be demanding if it were a charge of violence? The inference is that fifteen slaves know something, and that something is still a mystery. Or is it nothing mysterious and yet something connected with magic? You must admit one of these two alternatives: either the proceeding to which I admitted so many witnesses had nothing improper about it, or, if it had, it should not have been witnessed by so many. Now this magic of which you accuse me is, I am told, a crime in the eyes of the law, and was forbidden in remote antiquity by the Twelve Tables because in some incredible manner crops had been charmed away from one field to another. It is then as mysterious an art as it is loathly and horrible; it needs as a rule night-watches and concealing darkness, solitude absolute and murmured incantations, to hear which few free men are admitted, not to speak of slaves. And yet you will have it that there were fifteen slaves present on this occasion. Was it a marriage? Or any other crowded ceremony? Or a seasonable banquet? Fifteen slaves take part in a magic rite as though they had been created quindecimvirs for the performance of sacrifice! Is it likely that I should have permitted so large a number to be present on such an occasion, if they were too many to be accomplices? Fifteen free men form a borough, fifteen slaves a household, fifteen fettered serfs a chain-gang. Did I need such a crowd to help me by holding the lustral victims during the lengthy rite? No! the only victims you mentioned were hens! Were they to count the grains of incense? Or to knock Thallus down?

You assert also that by promising to heal her I inveigled to my house a free woman who suffered from the same disease as Thallus; that she, too, fell senseless as a result of my incantations. It appears to me that you are accusing a wrestler, not a magician, since you say that all who visited me had a fall. And yet Themison, who is a physician and who brought the woman for my inspection, denied, when you asked him, Maximus, that I had done anything to the woman other than ask her whether she heard noises in her ears, and if so, which ear suffered most. He added that she departed immediately after telling me that her right ear was most troubled in that way.

At this point, Maximus, although I have for the present been careful to abstain from praising you, lest I should seem to have flattered you with an eye to winning my case, yet I cannot help praising you for the astuteness of your questions. After they had spent much time in discussing these points and asserting that I had bewitched the woman, and after the doctor who was present on that occasion had denied that I had done so, you, with shrewdness more than human, asked them what profit I derived from my incantations They replied, 'The woman had a fit.' 'What then?' you asked, 'Did she die?' 'No,' they said. 'What is your point then? How did the fact of her having a fit profit Apuleius?'

That third question showed brilliant penetration and persistence. You knew that it was necessary to submit all facts to stringent examination of their causes, that often facts are admitted while motives remain to seek, and that the representatives of litigants are called pleaders of causes, because they set forth the causes of each particular act. To deny a fact is easy and needs no advocate, but it is far more arduous and difficult a task to demonstrate the rightness or wrongness of a given action. It is waste of time, therefore, to inquire whether a thing was done, when, even if it were done, no evil motive can be alleged. Under such circumstances, if no criminal motive is forthcoming, a good judge releases the accused from all further vexatious inquiry.

So now, since they have not proved that I either bewitched the woman or caused her to have a fit, I for my part will not deny that I examined her at the request of a physician; and I will tell you, Maximus, why I asked her if she had noises in her ears. I will do this not so much to clear myself of the charge which you, Maximus, have already decided to involve neither blame nor guilt, as to impart to you something worthy of your hearing and interesting to one of your erudition. I will tell you in as few words as possible. I have only to call your attention to certain facts. To instruct you would be presumption.

The philosopher Plato, in his glorious work, the Timaeus, sets forth with more than mortal eloquence the constitution of the whole universe. After discoursing with great insight on the three powers that make up man's soul, and showing with the utmost clearness the divine purpose that shaped our various members, he treats of the causes of all diseases under three heads. The first cause lies in the elements of the body, when the actual qualities of those elements, moisture and cold and their two opposites, fail to harmonize. That comes to pass when one of these elements assumes undue proportions or moves from its proper place. The second cause of disease lies in the vitiation of those components of the body which, though formed out of the simple elements, have coalesced in such a manner as to have a specific character of their own, such as blood, entrails, bone, marrow, and the various substances made from the blending of each of these. Thirdly, the concretion in the body of various juices, turbid vapours, and dense humours is the last provocative of sickness.

Of these causes that which contributes most to epilepsy, the disease of which I set out to speak, is a condition when the flesh is so melted by the noxious influence of fire as to form a thick and foaming humour. This generates a vapour, and the heat of the air thus compressed within the body causes a white and eruptive ferment. If this ferment succeeds in escaping from the body, it is dispersed in a manner that is repulsive rather than dangerous. For it causes an eczema to break out upon the surface of the skin of the breast and mottles it with all kinds of blotches. But the person to whom this happens is never again attacked with epilepsy, and so he rids himself of a most sore disease of the spirit at the price of a slight disfigurement of the body.

But if, on the other hand, this dangerous corruption be contained within the body and mingle with the black bile, and so run fiercely through every vein, and then working its way upwards to the head flood the brain with its destructive stream, it straightway weakens that royal part of man's spirit which is endowed with the power of reason and is enthroned in the head of man, that is its citadel and palace. For it overwhelms and throws into confusion those channels of divinity and paths of wisdom. During sleep it makes less havoc, but when men are full of meat and wine it makes its presence somewhat unpleasantly felt by a choking sensation, the herald of epilepsy. But if it reaches such strength as to attack the heads of men when they are wide awake, then their minds grow dull with a sudden cloud of stupefaction and they fall to the ground, their bodies swooning as in death, their spirit fainting within them. Men of our race have styled it not only the 'Great sickness' and the 'Comitial sickness', but also the 'Divine sickness', in this resembling the Greeks, who call it hiera nosos, the holy sickness. The name is just; for this sickness does outrage to the rational part of the soul, which is by far the most holy.

You recognize, Maximus, the theory of Plato, as far as I have been able to give it a lucid explanation in the time at my disposal. I put my trust in him when he says that the cause of epilepsy is the overflowing of this pestilential humour into the head. My inquiry therefore was, I think, reasonable when I asked the woman whether her head felt heavy, her neck numb, her temples throbbing, her ears full of noises. The fact that she acknowledged these noises to be more frequent in her right ear was proof that the disease had gone home. For the right-hand organs of the body are the strongest, and therefore their infection with the disease leaves small hope of recovery. Indeed Aristotle has left it on record in his Problems that whenever in the case of epileptics the disease begins on the right side, their cure is very difficult. It would be tedious were I to repeat the opinion of Theophrastus also on the subject of epilepsy. For he has left a most excellent treatise on convulsions. He asserts, however, in another book on the subject of animals ill-disposed towards mankind, that the skins of newts — which like other reptiles they shed at fixed intervals for the renewal of their youth — form a remedy for fits. But unless you snatch up the skin as soon as it be shed, they straightway turn upon it and devour it, whether from a malign foreknowledge of its value to men or from a natural taste for it.

I have mentioned these things, I have been careful to quote the arguments of renowned philosophers, and to mention the books where they are to be found, and have avoided any reference to the works of physicians or poets, that my adversaries may cease to wonder that philosophers have learnt the causes of remedies and diseases in the natural course of their researches.

Well then, since this woman was brought to be examined by me in the hope that she might be cured, and since it is clear both from the evidence of the physician who brought her and from the arguments I have just set forth that such a course was perfectly right, my opponents must needs assert that it is the part of a magician and evildoer to heal disease, or, if they do not dare to say that, must confess that their accusations in regard to this epileptic boy and woman are false, absurd, and indeed epileptic.

Yes, Aemilianus, if you would hear the truth, you are the real sufferer from the falling sickness, so often have your false accusations failed and cast you helpless to the ground. Bodily collapse is no worse than intellectual, and it is as important to keep one's head as to keep one's feet, while it is as unpleasant to be loathed by this distinguished gathering as to be spat upon in one's own chamber. But you perhaps think yourself sane because you are not confined within doors, but follow the promptings of your madness whithersoever it lead you: and yet compare your frenzy with that of Thallus; you will find that there is but little to choose between you, save that Thallus confines his frenzy to himself, while you direct yours against others; Thallus distorts his eyes, you distort the truth; Thallus contracts his hands convulsively, you not less convulsively contract with your advocates; Thallus dashes himself against the pavement, you dash yourself against the judgement-seat. In a word, whatever he does, he does in his sickness erring unconsciously; but you, wretch, commit your crimes with full knowledge and with your eyes open, such is the vehemence of the disease that inspires your actions. You bring false accusations as though they were true; you charge men with doing what has never been done; though a man's innocence be clear to you as daylight, you denounce him as though he were guilty.

Nay, further, though I had almost forgotten to mention it, there are certain things of which you confess your ignorance, and which nevertheless you make material for accusation as though you knew all about them. You assert that I kept something mysterious wrapped up in a handkerchief among the household gods in the house of Pontianus. You confess your ignorance as to what may have been the nature or appearance of this object; you further admit that no one ever saw it, and yet you assert that it was some instrument of magic. You are not to be congratulated on this method of procedure. Your accusation reveals no shrewdness, and has not even the merit of impudence. Do not think so for a moment. No! It shows naught save the ill-starred madness of an embittered spirit and the pitiable fury of cantankerous old age.

The words you used in the presence of so grave and perspicacious a judge amounted to something very like this. 'Apuleius kept certain things wrapped in a cloth among the household gods in the house of Pontianus. Since I do not know what they were, I therefore argue that they were magical. I beg you to believe what I say, because I am talking of that of which I know nothing.' What a wonderful argument, in itself an obvious refutation of the charge. 'It must have been this, because I do not know what it was.' You are the only person hitherto discovered who knows that which he does not know. You so far surpass all others in folly, that whereas philosophers of the most keen and penetrating intellect assert that we should not trust even the objects that we see, you make statements about things which you have never seen or heard.

If Pontianus still lived and you were to ask him what the cloth contained, he would reply that he did not know. There is the freedman who still has charge of the keys of the place; he is one of your witnesses, but he says that he has never examined these objects, although, as the servant responsible for the books kept there, he opened and shut the doors almost daily, continually entered the room, not seldom in my company but more often alone, and saw the cloth lying on the table unprotected by seal or cord. Quite natural, was it not? Magical objects were concealed in the cloth, and for that reason I took little care for its safe custody, but left it about anyhow for any one to examine and inspect, if he liked, or even to carry it away! I entrusted it to the custody of others, I left it to others to dispose of at their pleasure!

What credence do you expect us to give you after this? Are we to believe that you, on whom I have never set eyes save in this court, know that of which Pontianus, who actually lived under the same roof, was ignorant? Or shall we believe that you, who have never so much as approached the room where they were placed, have seen what the freedman never saw, although he had every opportunity to inspect them during the sedulous performance of his duties?

Suppose that what you never saw was such as you say. Yet, you fool, if this very day you had succeeded in getting that handkerchief into your hands, I should deny the magical nature of whatever you might produce from it.

I give you full leave; invent what you like, rack your memory and your imagination to discover something that might conceivably seem to be of a magical nature. Even then, should you succeed in so doing, I should argue the point with you. I should say that the object in question had been substituted by you for the original, or that it had been given as a remedy, or that it was a sacred emblem that had been placed in my keeping, or that a vision had bidden me to carry it thus. There are a thousand other ways in which I might refute you with perfect truth and without giving any explanation which is abnormal or lies outside the limits of common observation. You are now demanding that a circumstance, which, even if it were proved up to the hilt, would not prejudice me in the eyes of a good judge, should be fatal to me when, as it is, it rests on vague suspicion, uncertainty, and ignorance.

You will perhaps, as is your wont, say, 'What, then, was it that you wrapped in a linen cloth and were so careful to deposit with the household gods?' Really, Aemilianus! Is this the way you accuse your victims? You produce no definite evidence yourself, but ask the accused for explanations of everything.' 'Why do you search for fish?' 'Why did you examine a sick woman?' 'What had you hidden in your handkerchief?' Did you come here to accuse me or to ask me questions? If to accuse me, prove your charges yourself; if to ask questions, do not anticipate the truth by expressing opinions on that concerning which your ignorance compels you to inquire.

If this precedent is followed, if there is no necessity for the accuser to prove anything, but on the contrary he is given every facility for asking questions of the accused, there is not a man in all the world but will be indicted on some charge or other. In fact, everything that he has ever done will be used as a handle against any man who is charged with sorcery. Have you written a petition on the thigh of some statue? You are a sorcerer! Else why did you write it? Have you breathed silent prayers to heaven in some temple? You are a sorcerer! Else tell us what you asked for? Or take the contrary line. You uttered no prayer in some temple! You are a sorcerer! Else why did you not ask the gods for something? The same argument will be used if you have made some votive dedication, or offered sacrifice, or carried sprigs of some sacred plant. The day will fail me if I attempt to go through all the different circumstances of which, on these lines, the false accuser will demand an explanation. Above all, whatever object he has kept concealed or stored under lock and key at home will be asserted by the same argument to be of a magical nature, or will be dragged from its cupboard into the light of the law-court before the seat of judgement.

I might discourse at greater length on the nature and importance of such accusations, on the wide range for slander that this path opens for Aemilianus, on the floods of perspiration that this one poor handkerchief will cause his innocent victims. But I will follow the course I have already pursued. I will acknowledge what there is no necessity for me to acknowledge, and will answer Aemilianus' questions. You ask, Aemilianus, what I had in that handkerchief.

Although I might deny that I had deposited any handkerchief of mine in Pontianus' library, or even admitting that it was true enough that I did so deposit it, I might still deny that there was anything wrapped up in it. If I should take this line, you have no evidence or argument whereby to refute me, for there is no one who has ever handled it, and only one freedman, according to your own assertion, who has ever seen it. Still, as far as I am concerned I will admit the cloth to have been full to bursting. Imagine yourself, please, to be on the brink of a great discovery, like the comrades of Ulysses who thought they had found a treasure when they stole the bag that contained all the winds. Would you like me to tell you what I had wrapped up in a handkerchief and entrusted to the care of Pontianus' household gods? You shall have your will.

I have been initiated into various of the Greek mysteries, and preserve with the utmost care certain emblems and mementoes of my initiation with which the priests presented me. There is nothing abnormal or unheard of in this. Those of you here present who have been initiated into the mysteries of father Liber alone, know what you keep hidden at home, safe from all profane touch and the object of your silent veneration. But I, as I have said, moved by my religious fervour and my desire to know the truth, have learned mysteries of many a kind, rites in great number, and diverse ceremonies. This is no invention on the spur of the moment; nearly three years since, in a public discourse on the greatness of Aesculapius delivered by me during the first days of my residence at Oea, I made the same boast and recounted the number of the mysteries I knew. That discourse was thronged, has been read far and wide, is in all men's hands, and has won the affections of the pious inhabitants of Oea not so much through any eloquence of mine as because it treats of Aesculapius.

Will anyone, who chances to remember it, repeat the beginning of that particular passage in my discourse? You hear, Maximus, how many voices supply the words. I will order this same passage to be read aloud, since by the courteous expression of your face you show that you will not be displeased to hear it.

Can anyone, who has the least remembrance of the nature of religious rites, be surprised that one who has been initiated into so many holy mysteries should preserve at home certain talismans associated with these ceremonies, and should wrap them in a linen cloth, the purest of coverings for holy things? For wool, produced by the most stolid of creatures and stripped from the sheep's back, the followers of Orpheus and Pythagoras are for that very reason forbidden to wear as being unholy and unclean. But flax, the purest of all growths and among the best of all the fruits of the earth, is used by the holy priests of Egypt, not only for clothing and raiment, but as a veil for sacred things.

And yet I know that some persons, among them that fellow Aemilianus, think it a good jest to mock at things divine. For I learn from certain men of Oea who know him, that to this day he has never prayed to any god or frequented any temple, while if he chances to pass any shrine, he regards it as a crime to raise his hand to his lips in token of reverence. He has never given firstfruits of crops or vines or flocks to any of the gods of the farmer, who feed him and clothe him; his farm holds no shrine, no holy place, nor grove. But why do I speak of groves or shrines? Those who have been on his property say they never saw there one stone where offering of oil has been made, one bough where wreaths have been hung. As a result, two nicknames have been given him: he is called Charon, as I have said, on account of his truculence of spirit and of countenance, but he is also — and this is the name he prefers — called Mezentius, because he despises the gods. I therefore find it the easier to understand that he should regard my list of initiations in the light of a jest. It is even possible that, thanks to his rejection of things divine, he may be unable to induce himself to believe that it is true that I guard so reverently so many emblems and relics of mysterious rites.

But what Mezentius may think of me, I do not care a straw; to others I make this announcement clearly and unshrinkingly: if any of you that are here present had any part with me in these same solemn ceremonies, give a sign and you shall hear what it is I keep thus. For no thought of personal safety shall induce me to reveal to the uninitiated the secrets that I have received and sworn to conceal.

I have, I think, Maximus, said enough to satisfy the most prejudiced of men and, as far as the handkerchief is concerned, have cleared myself of every speck of guilt. I shall run no risk in passing from the suspicions of Aemilianus to the evidence of Crassus, which my accusers read out next as if it were of the utmost importance.

You heard them read from a written deposition, the evidence of a gorging brute, a hopeless glutton, named Junius Crassus, that I performed certain nocturnal rites at his house in company with my friend Appius Quintianus, who had taken lodgings there. This, mark you, Crassus says that he discovered (in spite of the fact that he was as far away as Alexandria at the time!) from finding the feathers of birds and traces of the smoke of a torch. I suppose that while he was enjoying a round of festivities at Alexandria — for Crassus is one who is ready even to encroach upon the daylight with his gluttonies — I suppose, I say, that there from his reeking-tavern he espied, with eye keen as any fowler's, feathers of birds wafted towards him from his house, and saw the smoke of his home rising far off from his ancestral rooftree. If he saw this with his eyes, he saw even further than Ulysses prayed and yearned to see. For Ulysses spent years in gazing vainly from the shore to see the smoke rising from his home, while Crassus during a few months' absence from home succeeded, without the least difficulty, in seeing this same smoke as he sat in a wine-shop! If, on the other hand, it was his nose that discerned the smoke, he surpasses hounds and vultures in the keenness of his sense of smell. For what hound, what vulture hovering in the Alexandrian sky, could sniff out anything so far distant as Oea? Crassus is, I admit, a gourmand of the first order, and an expert in all the varied flavours of kitchen-smoke, but in view of his love of drinking, his only real title to fame, it would have been easier to reach him at Alexandria for the fumes of his wine rather than the fumes of his chimney.

Even he saw that this would pass belief. For he is said to have sold this evidence before eight in the morning while he was still fasting from food and drink! And so he wrote that he had made his discovery in the following manner. On his return from Alexandria he went straight to his house, which Quintianus had by this time left. There in the entrance-hall he came across a large quantity of birds' feathers: the walls, moreover, were blackened with soot. He asked the reason of this from the slave whom he had left at Oea, and the latter informed him of the nocturnal rites carried out by myself and Quintianus.

What an ingenious lie! What a probable invention! That I, had I wished to do anything of the sort, should have done it there rather than in my own house! That Quintianus, who is supporting me here today, and whom I mention with the greatest respect and honour for the close love that binds him to me, for his deep erudition and consummate eloquence, that this same Quintianus, supposing him to have dined off some birds or, as they assert, killed them for magical purposes, should have had no slave to sweep up the feathers and throw them out of doors! Or further that the smoke should have been strong enough to blacken the walls and that Quintianus should have suffered such defacement of his bedroom for as long as he lived there! Nonsense, Aemilianus! There is no probability in the story, unless indeed Crassus on his return went not to the bedroom, but after his fashion made straight for the kitchen.

And what made his slave suspect that the walls had been blackened by night in particular? Was it the colour of the smoke? Does night smoke differ from day smoke in being darker? And why did so suspicious and conscientious a slave allow Quintianus to leave the house before having it cleaned? Why did those feathers lie like lead and await the arrival of Crassus for so long? Let not Crassus accuse his slave. It is much more likely that he himself fabricated this mendacious nonsense about feathers and soot, being unable even in his evidence to divorce himself further from his kitchen.

And why did you read out this evidence from a written deposition? Where in the world is Crassus? Has he returned to Alexandria out of disgust at the state of his house? Is he washing his walls? Or, as is more likely, is the glutton feeling ill after his debauch? I myself saw him yesterday here at Sabrata belching in your face, Aemilianus, in the most conspicuous manner in the middle of the market-place. Pray, Maximus, ask your slaves whose duty it is to keep you informed of people's names — although, I admit, Crassus is better known to the keepers of taverns — yet ask them, I say, whether they have ever seen Junius Crassus, a citizen of Oea, in this place. They will answer 'yes'. Let Aemilianus then produce this most admirable young man on whose testimony he relies.

You notice the time of day. I tell you that Crassus has long since been snoring in a drunken slumber or has taken a second bathe and is now evaporating the sweat of intoxication at the bath that he may be equal to a fresh drinking bout after supper. He presents himself in writing only. That is the way he speaks to you, Maximus. Even he is not so dead to sense of shame as to be able to lie to your face without a blush. But there is perhaps another reason for his absence. He may have been unable to abstain from drunkenness sufficiently long to keep sober against this moment.

Or it may be that Aemilianus took good care not to subject him to your severe and searching gaze, lest you should damn the brute with his close-shaven cheeks and his disgusting appearance by a mere glance at his face, when you saw a young man with his features stripped of the beard and hair that should adorn them, his eyes heavy with wine, his lids swollen, his grin, his slobbering lips, his harsh voice, his trembling hands, his breath reeking of the cook-shop. He has long since devoured his fortune; nothing is left him of his patrimony save a house that serves him for the sale of his false witness, and never did he make a more remunerative contract than he has done with regard to this evidence he offers today. For he sold Aemilianus his drunken fictions for 3,000 sesterces, as every one at Oea is aware.

We all knew of this before it actually took place. I might have prevented the transaction by denouncing it, but I knew that so foolish a lie would be prejudicial to Aemilianus, who wasted his money to secure it, rather than to myself, who treated it with the contempt it deserved. I wished not only that Aemilianus should lose his money, but that Crassus should have his reputation ruined by his disgraceful perjury. It was but the day before yesterday that the transaction took place in the most open manner at the house of Rufinus, of whom I shall soon have something to say. Rufinus and Calpurnianus acted as middlemen and entreated him to comply to their wishes. The former carried out the task with all the more readiness because he was certain that his wife, at whose misconduct he knowingly connives, would be sure to recover from Crassus a large proportion of his fee for perjury.

I noticed that you also, Maximus, as soon as this written evidence was produced, suspected with your usual acuteness that they had formed a league and conspiracy against me; and I saw from your face that the whole affair excited your disgust. Finally my accusers, in spite of their being paragons of audacity and monsters of shamelessness, noticed that Crassus' evidence smelled after faex and did not dare to read it out in full or to build anything upon it. I have mentioned these facts not because I am afraid of these dreadful feathers and stains of soot — least of all with you to judge me — but that Crassus might meet with due punishment for having sold mere smoke to a helpless rustic like Aemilianus.

And after all this, they have also come up, on reading Pudentilla's letters, concerning the manufacture of a seal. This seal, they assert, I had fashioned of the rarest wood by some secret process for purposes of the black art. They add that, although it is loathly and horrible to look upon, being in the form of a skeleton, I yet give it especial honour and call it in the Greek tongue, basileus, my king. I think I am right in saying that I am following the various stages of their accusation in due order and reconstructing the whole fabric of their slander detail by detail.

Now how can the manufacture of this seal have been secret, as you assert, when you are sufficiently well acquainted with the maker to have summoned him to appear in court? Here is Cornelius Saturninus, the artist, a man whose skill is famous among his townsfolk and whose character is above reproach. A little while back, in answer, Maximus, to your careful cross-examination, he explained the whole sequence of events in the most convincing and truthful manner. He said that I visited his shop and, after looking at many geometrical patterns all carved out of boxwood in the most cunning and ingenious manner, was so much attracted by his skill that I asked him to make me certain mechanical devices and also begged him to make me the image of some god to which I might pray after my custom. The particular god and the precise material I left to his choice, my only stipulation being that it should be made of wood. He therefore first attempted to work in boxwood. Meanwhile, during my absence in the country, Sicinius Pontianus, my step-son, wishing it to be made for me, procured some ebony tablets from that excellent lady Capitolina and brought them to his shop, exhorting him to make what I had ordered out of this rarer and more durable material: such a gift, he said, would be most gratifying to me. Our artist did as Pontianus suggested, as far as the size of the ebony tablets permitted. By careful dove-tailing of minute portions of the tablets he succeeded in making a small figure of Mercury.

You heard all the evidence just as I repeat it. Moreover, it receives exact confirmation from the answers given to you in cross-examination by Capitolina's son, a youth of the most excellent character, who is here in court today. He said that Pontianus asked for the tablets, that Pontianus took them to the artist Saturninus. Nor does he deny that Pontianus received the completed signet from Saturninus and afterwards gave it me.

All these things have been openly and manifestly proved. What remains, in which any suspicion of sorcery can lie concealed? Nay, what is there that does not absolutely convict you of obvious falsehood? You said that the seal was of secret manufacture, whereas Pontianus, a distinguished member of the equestrian order, gave the commission for it. The figure was carved in public by Saturninus as he sat in his shop. He is a man of sterling character and recognized honesty. The work was assisted by the munificence of a distinguished married lady, and many both among the slaves and the acquaintances who frequented my house were aware both of the commission for the work and its execution. You were not ashamed falsely to pretend that I had searched high and low for the requisite wood through all the town, although you know that I was absent from Oea at that time, and although it has been proved that I gave a free hand as to the material.

Your third lie was that the figure which was made was the lean, eviscerated frame of a gruesome corpse, utterly horrible and ghastly as any ghost. If you had discovered such definite proof of my sorceries, why did you not insist on my producing it in court? Was it that you might have complete freedom for inventing lies in the absence of the subject of your slanders? If so, the opportunity afforded you for mendacity has been lost you, thanks to a certain habit of mine which comes in most opportunely. It is my wont wherever I go to carry with me the image of some god kept among my books and to pray to him on feast days with offerings of incense and wine and sometimes even of victims. When, therefore, I heard persistent though outrageously mendacious assertions that the figure I carried was that of a skeleton, I ordered some one to go and bring from my house my little image of Mercury, the same that Saturninus had made for me at Oea. You here, give it them! Let them see it, hold it, examine it. There you see the image which that scoundrel called a skeleton. Do you hear these cries of protest that arise from all present? Do you hear the condemnation of your lie? Are you not at last ashamed of all your slanders? Is this a skeleton, this a ghost, is this the familiar spirit you asserted it to be? Is this a magic symbol or one that is common and ordinary?

Take it, I beg you, Maximus, and examine it. It is good that a holy thing should be entrusted to hands as pure and pious as yours. See there, how fair it is to view, how full of all a wrestler's grace and vigour! How cheerful is the god's face, how comely the down that creeps on either side his cheeks, how the curled hair shows upon his head beneath the shadow of his hat's brim, how neatly the tiny pair of pinions project about his brows, how daintily the cloak is drawn about his shoulders! He who dares call this a skeleton, either never sees an image of a god or if he does ignores it. Indeed, he who thinks this to represent a ghost is evoking ghosts.

But in return for that lie, Aemilianus, may that same god who goes between the lords of heaven and the lords of hell grant you the hatred of the gods of either world and ever send to meet you the shadows of the dead with all the shades, with all the fiends, with all the spectrets, with all the ghosts of all the world, and thrust upon your eyes all the terror that walks by night, all the dread dwellers in the tomb, all the horrors of the sepulchre, although your age and character have brought you near enough to them already.

But we of the family of Plato know naught save what is bright and joyous, majestic and heavenly and of the world above us. Nay, in its zeal to reach the heights of wisdom, the Platonic school has explored regions higher than heaven itself and has stood triumphant on the outer circumference of this our universe. Maximus knows that I speak truth, for in his careful study of the Phaedrus he has read of the 'place being builded on heaven's back.' Maximus also clearly understands — I am now going to reply to your accusation about the name — who he is whom not

I but Plato was first to call the 'King'. 'All things,' he says, 'depend upon the King of all things and for him only all things exist.' Maximus knows who that 'King' is, even the cause and reason and primal origin of all nature, the lord and father of the soul, the eternal saviour of all that lives, the unwearying builder of his world. Yet he builds without labour, yet he saves without care, he is father without begetting, he knows no limitation of space or time or change, and therefore few may conceive and none may tell of his power.

I will even go out of my way to aggravate the suspicion of sorcery; I will not tell you, Aemilianus, who it is that I worship as my king. Even if the proconsul should ask me himself who my god is, I am dumb.

About the name I have said enough for the present. For the rest I know that some of my audience are anxious to hear why I wanted the figure made not of silver or gold, but only of wood, though I think that their desire springs not so much from their anxiety to see me cleared of guilt as from eagerness for knowledge. They would like to have this last doubt removed, even although they see that I have amply rebutted all suspicion of any crime. Listen, then, you who would know, but listen with all the sharpness and attention that you may, for you are to hear the very words that Plato wrote in his old age in the last book of the Laws.

The man of moderate means when he makes offerings to the gods should do so in proportion to his means. Now, earth and the household hearths of all men are holy to all the gods. Let no one therefore dedicate any shrines to the gods over and above these.

He forbids this with the purpose of preventing men from venturing to build private shrines; for he thinks that the public temples suffice his citizens for the purposes of sacrifice. He then continues,

Gold and silver in other cities, whether in the keeping of private persons or of temples, are invidious possessions; ivory taken from a body wherefrom the life has passed is not a welcome offering; iron and bronze are instruments of war. Whatsoever a man dedicates, let it be of wood and wood only, or if it be of stone, of stone only.

The general murmur of assent shows, Maximus, and you, gentlemen, who have the honour to assist him, that I am adjudged to have made admirable use of Plato, not only as a guide in life, but as an advocate in court, to whose laws, as you see, I obey.

It is now time for me to turn first and foremost to the letters of Pudentilla, or rather to retrace the whole course of events a little further back still. For I desire to make it abundantly clear that I, whom they keep accusing of having forced my way into Pudentilla's house solely through love of money, ought really never to have come near that house, had the thought of money ever crossed my mind. My marriage has for many reasons brought me the reverse of prosperity and, but for the fact that my wife's virtues are compensation for any number of disadvantages, it would be contrary to my interests.

Disappointment and envy are the sole causes that have involved me in this trial, and even before that gathered many mortal perils about my path. What motiva for resentment has Aemilianus against me, even assuming him to be correctly informed when he accuses me of magic? No least word of mine has ever injured him in such a way as to give him the appearance of pursuing a just revenge. It is certainly no lofty ambition that prompts him to accuse me, ambition such as fired Marcus Antonius to accuse Cnaeus Carbo, Caius Mucius to accuse Aulus Albucius, Publius Sulpicius to accuse Cnaeus Norbanus, Caius Furius to accuse Marcus Aquilius, Caius Curio to accuse Quintus Metellus. They were young men of admirable education and were led by ambition to undertake these accusations as the first step in a forensic career, that by the conduct of some 'cause celebre' they might make themselves a name among their fellow citizens. This privilege was conceded by antiquity to young men just entering public life as a means of winning glory for their youthful genius. The custom has long since become obsolete, but even if the practice were still common, it would not apply to Aemilianus. It would not have been becoming to him to make any display of his eloquence, for he is rude and unlettered; nor to show a passion for renown, since he is a mere barbarian bumpkin; nor thus to open his career as an advocate, for he is an old man on the brink of the grave. The only hypothesis creditable to him would be that he is perhaps giving an example of his austerity of character and has undertaken this accusation through sheer hatred of wrongdoing and to assert his own integrity. But I should hardly accept such an hypothesis even in the case of a greater Aemilianus, not our African friend here, but the conqueror of Africa and Numantia, who held, moreover, the office of censor at Rome. Much less will I believe that this dull blockhead, I will not say, hates sin, but recognizes it when he sees it.

What then was his motive? It is as clear as day to any one that envy is the sole motive that has spurred him and Herennius Rufinus, his instigator — of whom I shall have more to say later — and the rest of my enemies, to fabricate these false charges of sorcery.

Well, there are five points which I must discuss. If I remember aright, their accusations as regards Pudentilla were as follows. Firstly, they said that after the death of her first husband she resolutely set her face against re-marriage, but was seduced by my incantations. Secondly, there are her letters, which they regard as an admission that I used sorcery. Thirdly and fourthly, they object that she made a lovematch at the advanced age of sixty and that the marriage contract was sealed not in the town but at a country house. Lastly, there is the most invidious of all these accusations, namely, that which concerns the dowry. It is into this charge they have put all their force and all their venom; it is this that vexes them most of all. They assert that at the very outset of our wedded life I forced my devoted wife in the absolute seclusion of her country house to make over to me a large dowry.

I will show that all these statements are so false, so worthless, so unsubstantial, and I shall refute them so easily and unquestionably, that in good truth, Maximus, and you, gentlemen, his assessors, I fear you may think that I have suborned my accusers to bring these charges, that I might have the opportunity of publicly dispelling the hatred of which I am the victim. I will ask you to believe now what you will understand when the facts are before you, that I shall need to put out all my strength to prevent you from thinking that such a baseless accusation is a cunning device of my own rather than a stupid enterprise of my enemies.

I shall now briefly retrace events and force Aemilianus himself to admit, whenhe has heard the facts, that his envy was groundless and that he has strayed far from the truth. In the meantime I beg you, as you have already done, or if possible yet more than you have already done, to give the best of your attention to me as I trace the whole case to its fount and source.

Aemilia Pudentilla, now my wife, was once the wife of a certain Sicinius Amicus. By him she had two sons, Pontianus and Pudens. These two boys were left by their father's death under the guardianship of their paternal grandfather — for Amicus predeceased his father — and were brought up by their mother with remarkable care and affection for about fourteen years. She was in the flower of her age, and it was not of her own choosing that she remained a widow for so long. But the boys' grandfather was eager that she should, in spite of her reluctance, take his son, Sicinius Clarus, for her second husband and with this in view kept all other suitors at a distance. He further threatened her that if she married elsewhere he would by his will exclude her sons from the possession of any of their father's heritage. When she saw that nothing could move him to alter the condition that he had laid down, such was her wisdom, and so admirable her maternal affection, that to prevent her sons' interests suffering any damage in this respect, she made a contract of marriage with Sicinius Clarus in accordance with her father-in-law's bidding, but by various evasions managed to avoid the marriage until the boys' grandfather died, leaving them as his heirs, with the result that Pontianus, the elder son, became his brother's guardian.

She was now freed from all embarrassment, and being sought in marriage by many distinguished persons resolved to remain a widow no longer. The dreariness of her solitary life she might have borne, but her bodily infirmities had become intolerable. This chaste and saintly lady, after so many years of blameless widowhood, without even a breath of scandal, owing to her long absence from a husband's embraces, began to suffer internal pains so severe that they brought her to the brink of the grave. Doctors and wise women agreed that the disease had its origin in her long widowhood, that the evil was increasing daily and her sickness steadily assuming a more serious character; the remedy was that she should marry before her youth finally departed from her.

There were many who welcomed this recommendation, but none more so than that fellow Aemilianus, who a little while back asserted with the most unhesitating mendacity that Pudentilla had never thought of marriage until I compelled her to be mine by my exercise of the black art; that I alone had been found to outrage the virgin purity of her widowhood by incantations and love philtres. I have often heard it said with truth that a liar should have a good memory. Had you forgotten, Aemilianus, that before I came to Oea, you wrote to her son Pontianus, who had then attained to man's estate and was pursuing his studies at Rome, suggesting that she should marry?

Give me the letter, or better give it to Aemilianus and let him refute himself in his own voice with his own words. Is this your letter? Why do you turn pale? We know you are past blushing. Is this your signature? Read a little louder, please, that all may realize how his written words belie his speech and how much more he is at variance with himself than with me.

Did you, Aemilianus, write what has just been read out? 'I know that she is willing to marry and that she ought to do so, but I do not know the object of her choice.' You were right there. You knew nothing about it. For Pudentilla, though she admitted that she wished to marry again, said nothing to you about her suitor. She knew the intrusive malignity of your nature too well. But you still expected her to marry your brother Clarus and were induced by your false hopes to go further and to urge her son to assent to the match.

And of course, if she had wedded Clarus, a boorish and decrepit old man, you would have asserted that she had long desired to marry him of her own free will without the intervention of any magic. But now that she has married a young man of the elegance which you attribute to him, you say that she had always refused to marry and must have done so under compulsion! You did not know, you villain, that the letter you had written on the subject was being preserved, you did not know that you would be convicted by your own testimony. The fact is that Pudentilla, knowing your changeableness and unreliability no less than your shamelessness and mendacity, rather than forward the letter preferred to keep it as clear evidence of your intentions.

Furthermore, she wrote a letter of her own on the same subject to her son Pontianus at Rome, in which she gave full reasons for her determination. She told him pretty fully about the state of her health; there was no longer any reason for her to persist in remaining a widow; she had so remained for thus long and had sacrificed her health solely to procure him the inheritance of his grandfather's fortune, a fortune to which she had by the exercise of the greatest care made considerable additions; Pontianus himself was now by the grace of heaven ripe for marriage and his brother for the garb of manhood; she begged them to suffer her at length to solace her lonely existence and to relieve her ill health; they need have no fears as to her final choice or as to her motherly affection; she would still be as a wife what she had been as a widow. I will order a copy of this letter to her son to be read aloud.

This letter makes it, I think, sufficiently clear that it needed no incantations of mine to move Pudentilla from her resolve to remain a widow, but that she had been for some time by no means averse to marriage, when she chose me — it may be in preference to others. I cannot see why such a choice by so excellent a woman should be brought against me as matter for reproach rather than honour. But I admit feeling surprise that Aemilianus and Rufinus should be annoyed at the lady's decision, when those who were actually suitors for her hand acquiesce in her preference for myself.

She was indeed guided in making her choice less by her personal inclination than by the advice of her son, a fact which Aemilianus cannot deny. For Pontianus on receiving his mother's letter hastily flew hither from Rome, fearing that, if the man of her choice proved to be avaricious, she might, as often happens, transfer her whole fortune to the house of her new husband. This anxiety tormented him not a little. All his own expectations of wealth together with those of his brother depended on his mother. His grandfather had left but a moderate fortune, his mother possessed 4,000,000 sesterces. Of this sum, it is true, she owed a considerable portion to her sons, but they had no security for this, relying, naturally enough, on her word alone. He gave but silent expression to his fears; he did not venture to show any open opposition for fear of seeming to distrust her.

Things being in this delicate position owing to the mother's request and the son's fear, chance or destiny brought me to Oea on my way to Alexandria. Did not my respect for my wife prevent me, I would say 'Would God it had never happened.' It was winter when this occurred. Overcome by the fatigues of the journey, I was laid up for a considerable number of days in the house of my friends the Appii, whom I name to show the affection and esteem with which I regard them. There Pontianus came to see me; for not so very long before certain common friends had introduced him to me at Athens, and we had afterwards lodged together and come to know each other intimately. He greeted me with the utmost courtesy, inquired anxiously after my health, and touched dexterously on the subject of love. For he thought that he had found an ideal husband for his mother to whom he could without the slightest risk entrust the whole fortune of the house. At first he sounded me as to my inclinations in somewhat ambiguous language, and seeing that I was desirous of resuming my journey and was not in the least disposed to take a wife, he begged me at any rate to remain at Oea for a little while, as he himself was desirous of travelling with me.

Since my physical infirmity had made it impossible for me to profit by the present winter, he urged that it would be well to wait for the next owing to the danger presented by the passage of the Syrtes and the risk of encountering wild beasts. His urgent entreaty induced my friends the Appii to allow me to leave them and to become his guest in his mother's house. I should find the situation healthier, he said, and should get a freer view of the sea — a special attraction in my eyes.

He had shown the greatest eagerness in inducing me to come to this decision, and strongly recommended his mother and his brother — that boy there — to my consideration. I gave them some help in our common studies and a marked intimacy sprang up between us. Meanwhile I gradually recovered my health. At the instance of my friends I gave a discourse in public. This took place in the basilica, which was thronged by a vast audience. I was greeted with many expressions of approval, the audience shouted 'bravo! bravo!' like one man, and besought me to remain and become a citizen of Oea. On the dispersal of the audience Pontianus approached me, and by way of prelude said that such universal enthusiasm was nothing less than a sign from heaven. He then revealed to me that it was his cherished design — with my permission — to bring about a match between myself and his mother, for whose hand there were many suitors. He added that I was the only friend in the world in whom he could put implicit trust and confidence. If I were to refuse to undertake such a responsibility, simply because it was no fair heiress that was offered me, but a woman of plain appearance nd the mother of children — if I were moved by these considerations and insisted on reserving myself for a more attractive and wealthier match, my behaviour would be unworthy of a friend and a philosopher.

It would take too long — even if I were willing to tell you what I replied and how long and how frequently we conversed on the subject, with how many pressing entreaties he plied me, never ceasing until he finally won my consent. I had had ample opportunity for observing Pudentilla's character, for I had lived for a whole year continually in her company and had realized how rich was her endowment of good qualities; but my desire for travel led me to desire to refuse the match as an impediment. But I soon began to love her for her virtues as ardently as though I had wooed her of my own initiative. Pontianus had also persuaded his mother to give me the preference over all her other suitors, and showed extraordinary eagerness for the marriage to take place at the earliest possible date. We could scarcely induce him to consent to the very briefest postponement to such time as he himself should have taken a wife and his brother in due course have assumed the garb of manhood. That done, we would be married at once.

Would to heaven it were possible without serious damage to my case to pass by what I have now to relate. I freely forgave Pontianus when he begged for pardon, and I have no wish to seem to reproach him now for the fickleness of his conduct. I acknowledge the truth of a circumstance brought against me by my accusers, I admit that Pontianus, after taking to himself a wife, broke his pledged word and suddenly changed his mind; that he tried to prevent the fulfilment of this project with no less obstinacy than he had shown zeal in forwarding it. He was ready to make any sacrifice, to go any lengths, to prevent our marriage taking place. Nevertheless this discreditable change of attitude, this deliberate quarrel with his mother, must not be laid to his charge, but to that of his father-in-law, Herennius Rufinus, whom you see before you, a man than whom no more worthless, wicked, and crime-stained soul lives upon this earth. I will — since I cannot avoid it — give a brief description of this man's character, using such moderation as I may, lest, if I pass him by in silence, the energy which he has shown in engineering this accusation against me should have been spent all in vain.

This is the man who poisoned that worthless boy against me, who is the prime mover in this accusation, who has hired advocates and bought witnesses. This is the furnace in which all this calumny has been forged, this the firebrand, this the scourge that has driven Aemilianus here to his task. He makes it his boast before all men in the most extravagant language that it is through his machinations that my indictment has been procured. In truth he has some reason for self-congratulation. For he is the organizer of every lawsuit, the deviser of every perjury, the architect of every lie, the seed-ground of every wickedness, the habitation of lust and gluttony, a brothel and a house of whores; the mark of every scandal since his earliest years; in boyhood, ere he became so hideously bald, the ready servant of his pederasts in the vilest vices; in youth a stage dancer limp and nerveless enough in all conscience, but, they tell me, clumsy and inartistic in his very effeminacy. He is said not to have possessed a single quality that should distinguish an actor, except for his indecency.

He is older now — God's curse upon him! I crave your pardon for my warmth of language. But his house is the dwelling-place of panders, his whole household foul with sin, himself a man of infamous character, his wife a harlot, his sons like their parents. His door night and day is battered with the kicks of wanton gallants, his windows loud with the sound of loose serenades, his dining-room wild with revel, his bedchambers the haunt of adulterers. For no one need fear to enter it save he who has no gift for the husband. Thus does he make an income from the shame of his own bed. Once he had been good at making money everywhere with his own body, now with that of wife. With none but him — it is not a lie! — with none but him most make the arrangements for a night with his wife. So here we have this well known collusion of husband and wife: whoever have brought a large sum to the woman are not checked by anyone and can leave as they wish. Whoever has come with less, are caught as adulterers, after a sign has been given; and as if they had come to school, they are not allowed to leave before they have 'written something.'

What else should the wretch do? He has lost a considerable fortune, though I admit that he only got that fortune unexpectedly through a fraudulent transaction on the part of his father. The latter, having borrowed money from a number of persons, preferred to keep their money at the cost of his own good name. Bills poured in on every side with demands for payment. Every one that met him laid hands on him as though he were a madman. 'Steady, now!' he says, stating that he cannot pay. So he resigned his golden rings and all the badges of his position in society and thus came to terms with his creditors. But he had by a most ingenious fraud transferred the greater part of his property to his wife, and so, although he himself was needy, ill-clad and protected by the very depth of his fall, managed to leave this same Rufinus — I am telling you the truth and nothing but the truth — no less than 3,000,000 sesterces to be squandered on riotous living. This was the sum that came to him unencumbered from his mother's property, over and above the daily dowry brought him by his wife. Yet all this money has been ravenously devoured by this glutton in a few short years, all this fortune has been destroyed by the infinite variety of his gormandizing; so that you might really think him to be afraid of seeming in any way to be the gainer by his father's dishonesty. This honourable fellow actually took care that what had been ill-gained should be ill-spent, nor was anything left him from his too ample fortune, save his depraved ambition and his boundless appetite.

His wife, however, was getting old and worn out and gave up the whole household to dishonour. But there was a daughter who, at her mother's instigation, was exhibited to all the wealthy young men, but in vain. To some of the suitors she was even given to try. Had she not come across so easy a victim as Pontianus, she would perhaps still have been sitting at home a widow who had never been a bride. Pontianus, in spite of urgent attempts on our part to dissuade him, gave her the right — false and illusory though it was — to be called a bride. He did this knowing that, but a short time before he married her, she had been deserted by a young man of good family to whom she had been previously betrothed, after he had had enough of her.

And so his new bride came to him, not as other brides come, but unabashed and undismayed, her virtue lost, her modesty gone, her bridal-veil a mockery. Cast off by her previous lover, she brought to her wedding the name without the purity of a maid. She rode in a litter carried by eight slaves. You who were present saw how impudently she made eyes at all the young and how immodestly she flaunted her charms. Who did not recognize her mother's pupil, when they saw her dyed lips, her rouged cheeks, and her lascivious eyes? Her dowry was borrowed, every penny of it, on the eve of her wedding, and was indeed greater than could be expected of so large and impoverished a family.

But though Rufinus' fortune is small, his hopes are boundless. With avarice rivalled only by his need he had already devoured Pudentilla's 4,000,000 in vain anticipation. With this in view he decided that I must be got out of the way, in order that he might find fewer obstacles in his attempt to hoodwink the weak Pontianus and the lonely Pudentilla. He began, therefore, to upbraid his son-in-law for having betrothed his mother to me. He urged him to draw back without delay from so perilous a path, while there was yet time; to keep his mother's fortune himself rather than deliberately transfer it to the keeping of a stranger. He threatened that, if he refused, he would take away his daughter, the device of an old hand to influence a young man in love.

To be brief, he so wrought upon the simple-minded young man, who was, moreover, a slave to the charms of his new bride, as to mould him to his will and move him from his purpose. Pontianus went to his mother and told her what Rufinus had said to him. But he made no impression on her steadfast character. On the contrary, she rebuked him for his fickleness and inconstancy, and it was no pleasant news he took back to his father-in-law. His mother had shown a firmness of purpose not to be expected of one of her placid disposition, and to make matters worse, his expostulations had made her angry, which was likely seriously to increase her obstinacy; in fact, she had finally replied, that it was no secret to her that his expostulations were instigated by Rufinus, a fact which made the support and assistance of a husband against his desperate greed all the more necessary to her.

When he heard this, the ruffian was stung to fury and burst into such wild and ungovernable rage that in the presence of her own son he heaped insults, such as he might have used to his own wife, on the purest and most modest of women. In the presence of many witnesses, whom, if you desire it, I will name, he loudly denounced her as a wanton and myself as a sorcerer and poisoner, threatening to murder me with his own hands. I can hardly restrain my anger, such fierce indignation fills my soul. That you, the most effeminate of men, should threaten any man with death at your hand! What hand? The hand of Philomela or Medea or Clytemnestra? Why, when you dance in those characters you show such contemptible timidity, you are so frightened at the sight of steel, that you will not even carry a property sword.

But I am digressing. Pudentilla, seeing to her astonishment that her son had fallen lower than she could have deemed possible, went into the country and by way of rebuke wrote him the notorious letter, in which, according to my accusers, she confessed that my magical practices had made her lose her reason and fall in love with me. And yet, Maximus, the day before yesterday at your command I took a copy of the letter in the presence of witnesses and of Pontianus' secretary. Aemilianus also was there and countersigned the copy. What is the result? In contradiction to my accusers' assertion everything is found to tell in my favour.

And yet, even if she had spoken somewhat strongly and had called me a magician, it would be a reasonable explanation that she had, in defending her conduct to her son, preferred to allege compulsion on my part rather than her own inclination. Is Phaedra the only woman whom love has driven to write a lying letter? Is it not rather a device common to all women that, when they have begun to feel strong desire for anything of this kind, they should prefer to make themselves out the victims of compulsion? But even supposing she had genuinely regarded me as a magician, would the mere fact of Pudentilla's writing to that effect be a reason for actually regarding me as a magician? You, with all your arguments and your witnesses and your diffuse eloquence, have failed to prove me a magician. Could she prove it with one word? A formal indictment, written and signed before a judge, is a far more weighty document than what is written in a private letter! Why do not you prove me a magician by my own deeds instead of having recourse to the mere words of another?

If your principle be followed, and whatever any one may have written in a letter under the influence of love or hatred be admitted as proof, many a man will be indicted on the wildest charges. 'Pudentilla called you a magician in her letter; therefore you are a magician!' If she had called me a consul, would that make me one? What if she had called me a painter, a doctor, or even an innocent man? Would you accept any of these statements, simply because she had made them? You would accept none of them. Yet it is a gross injustice to believe a person when he speaks evil of another and to refuse to believe him when he speaks well. It is a gross injustice that a letter should have power to destroy and not to save. - 'But,' says my accuser, 'she was out of her wits, she loved you distractedly.' I will grant it for the moment. But are all persons, who are the objects of love, magicians, just because the person in love with them chances to say so in a letter? If, indeed, Pudentilla wrote in a letter to another person what would clearly be prejudicial to myself, I think she could hardly have been in love with me at the moment in question.

Tell me now, what is your contention: was she mad or sane when she wrote? Sane, do you say? Then she was not the victim of magic. Insane? In that case she did not know what she was writing and must not be believed. Nay, even supposing her to have been insane, she would not have been aware of the fact. For just as to say 'I am silent' is to make a fool of oneself, since these very words actually break silence, and the act of speaking impugns the substance of one's speech, so it is even more absurd to say 'I am mad'. It cannot be true unless the speaker knows what he says, and he who knows what madness is, is ipso facto sane. For madness cannot know itself any more than blindness can see itself. Therefore Pudentilla was in possession of her senses, if she thought she was out of them. I could say more on this point, but enough of dialectic!

I will read out the letter which gives crying witness to a very different state of things and might indeed have been specially prepared to suit this particular trial. Take it and read it out until I interrupt.

Stop a moment before you go on to what follows. We have come to the crucial point. So far, Maximus, as far at any rate as I have noticed, the lady has made no mention of magic, but has merely repeated in the same order the statements which I quoted a short time ago about her long widowhood, the proposed remedy for her ill health, her desire to marry, the good report she had heard of me from Pontianus, his own advice that she should marry me in preference to others.

So much for what has been read. There remains a portion of the letter which, although like the first part it was written in my defence, also turns against me. For although it was specially written to rebut the charge of magic brought against me, a remarkable piece of ingenuity on the part of Rufinus has altered its meaning and brought me into discredit with certain citizens of Oea as being a proved sorcerer.

Maximus, you have heard much from the lips of others, you have learned yet more by reading, and your own personal experience has taught you not a little. But you will say that never yet have you come across such insidious cunning or such marvellous dexterity in crime. What Palamedes, what Sisyphus, what Eurybates or Phrynondas could ever have devised such guile? All those whom I have mentioned, together with all the notorious deceivers of history, would seem mere clowns and pantaloons, were they to attempt to match this one single instince of Rufinus' craftiness. O miracle of lies! O subtlety worthy of the prison and the stocks! Who could imagine that what was written as a defence could without the alteration of a single letter be transformed into an accusation! Good God! it is incredible. But I will make clear to you how the incredible came to pass.

The mother was rebuking her son because, after extolling me to her as a model of all the virtues, he now, at Rufinus' instigation, asserted that I was a magician. The actual words were as follows:

Apuleius is a magician and has bewitched me to love him! Come to me, then, while I am still in my senses.

These words, which I have quoted in Greek, have been selected by Rufinus and separated from their context. He has taken them round as a confession on the part of Pudentilla, and, with Pontianus at his side all dissolved in tears, has shown them through all the market-place, allowing men only to read that portion which I have just cited and suppressing all that comes before and after. His excuse was that the rest of the letter was too disgusting to be shown; it was sufficient that publicity should be given to Pudentilla's confession as to my sorcery.

What was the result? Everyone thought it probable enough. That very letter, which was written to clear my character, excited the most violent hatred against me amongst those who did not know the facts. This foul villain went rushing about in the midst of the market-place like any bacchanal; he kept opening the letter and proclaiming, 'Apuleius is a sorcerer! She herself describes her feelings and her sufferings! What more do you demand?' There was no one to take my part and reply, 'Give us the whole letter, please! Let me see it all, let me read it from beginning to end. There are many things which, produced apart from their context, may seem open to a slanderous inter-pretation. Any speech may be attacked, if a passage depending for its sense on what has preceded be robbed of its commencement, or if phrases be expunged at will from the place they logically occupy, or if what is written ironically be read out in such a tone as to make it seem a defamatory statement.'

With what justice this protest or words to that effect might have been uttered the actual order of the letter will show.

Now, Aemilianus, try to remember whether the following were not the words of which, together with myself, you took a copy in the presence of witnesses.

For since I desired to marry for the reasons of which I told you, you persuaded me to choose Apuleius in preference to all others, since you had a great admiration for him and were eager through me to become yet more intimate with him. But now that certain ill-natured persons have brought accusations against us and attempt to dissuade you, Apuleius has suddenly become a magician and has bewitched me to love him! Come to me, then, while I am still in my senses.

I ask you, Maximus, if letters — some of which are actually called vocal — could find a voice, if words, as poets say, could take them wings and fly, would they not, when Rufinus first made disingenuous excerpts from that letter, read but a few lines and deliberately said nothing of much that bore a more favourable meaning, would not the remaining letters have cried out that they were unjustly kept out of sight? Would not the words suppressed by Rufinus have flown from his hands and filled the whole market-place with tumult: 'they too had been sent by Pudentilla, they too had been entrusted with something to say; men should not give ear to a dishonest villain attempting to prove a lie by means of another's letter, but rather listen to them; Pudentilla never accused Apuleius of magic, while Rufinus' accusation was tantamount to an acquittal.' All these things were not said then, but now, when they are of more effectual service to me, their truth appears clearer than day. Rufinus, your cunning stands revealed, your fraud stares us in the face, your lies are laid bare; truth dethroned for a while rises once more and transcends slander as if from a bottomless pit.

You challenged me with Pudentilla's letter: with that letter I win the day. If you like to hear the conclusion, I will not grudge it you. Tell me, what were the words with which she ended the letter, that poor bewitched, lunatic, insane, infatuated lady?

I am not bewitched, I am not in love; it is my destiny.

Would you have anything more? Pudentilla throws your words in your teeth and publicly vindicates her sanity against your slanderous aspersions. The motive or necessity of her marriage, whichever it was, she now ascribes to fate, and between fate and magic there is a great gulf, indeed they have absolutely nothing in common. For if it be true that the destiny of each created thing is like a fierce torrent that may neither be stayed nor diverted, what power is left for magic drugs or incantations? Pudentilla, therefore, not only denied that I was a magician, but denied the very existence of magic. It is a good thing that Pontianus, following his usual custom, kept his mother's letter safe in its entirety: it is a good thing that the speed with which this case has been hurried on left you no opportunity for adding to that letter at your leisure. For this I have to thank you and your foresight, Maximus. You saw through their slanders from the beginning and hurried on the case that they might not gather strength as the days went by; you gave them no breathing space and wrecked their designs.

Suppose now that the mother, after her wont, had made confession of her passion for me in some private letter to her son. Was it just, Rufinus, was it consistent, I will not say with filial piety but with common humanity, that these letters should be circulated and, above all, published and proclaimed abroad by her own son? But perhaps I am no better than a fool to ask you to have regard for another's sense of decency when you have so long lost your own.

Why should I only complain of what is past? The present is equally distressing. To think that this unhappy boy should have been so corrupted by you as to read aloud in the proconsular court, before a man of such lofty character as Claudius Maximus, a letter from his mother, which he chooses to regard as amatory, and in the presence of the statues of the emperor Pius to accuse his mother of yielding to a shameful passion and reproach her with her amours? Who is there of such gentle temper, but that this would wake him to fury? Vilest of creatures, do you pry into your mother's heart in such matters, do you watch her glances, count her sighs, sound her affections, intercept her letters, and accuse her of being in love? Do you seek to discover what she does in the privacy of her own chamber, do you demand — I will not say that she should be above love affairs — but that she should cease to be a woman? Cannot you conceive the possibility that she should show any affection save the affection of a mother for her son? Ah! Pudentilla, you are unhappy in your offspring! Far better have been barren than have borne such children! Ill-omened were the long months through which you bore them in your womb and thankless your fourteen years of widowhood! The viper, I am told, reaches the light of day only by gnawing through its mother's womb; its parent must die before it is born. But your son is fullgrown and the wounds he deals are far bitterer, for they are inflicted on you while you yet live and see the light of day. He insults your reserve, he arraigns your modesty, he wounds you to the heart and outrages your dearest affections.

Is this the gratitude with which a dutiful son like yourself repays his mother for the life she gave him, for the inheritance she won him for her long fourteen years of seclusion? Is the result of your uncle's teaching this, that, if you were sure your sons would be like yourself, you should be afraid to take a wife? There is a well-known line

I hate the boy that's wise before his time.

Yes, and who would not loathe and detest a boy that is 'wicked before his time,' when he sees you, like some frightful portent, old in sin but young in years, with the bodily powers of a boy, yet deep in guilt, with the bright face of a child, but with wickedness such as might match grey hairs? Nay, the most offensive thing about him is that his pernicious deeds go scot free; he is too young to punish, yet old enough to do injury. Injury, did I say? No! crime, unfilial, black, monstrous, intolerable crime!

The Athenians, when they captured the correspondence of their enemy, Philip of Macedon, and the letters were being read in public one by one, out of reverence for the common rights of humanity forbade one letter to be read aloud, a letter addressed by Philip to his wife Olympias. They spared the enemy that they might not intrude on the privacy of husband and wife; they placed the law that is common to all mankind above the claims of private vengeance. So enemy dealt with enemy! And how have you dealt as son with his mother? You see how close is my parallel. Yet you read out aloud letters written by your mother which, according to your assertion, concern her love affairs, and you do so before this gathering here assembled, a gathering before which you would not dare to read the verses of some obscene poet, even if bidden to do so, but you would be restrained by some sense of shame. Nay, you would never have touched your mother's letters, had you ever been in touch with letters.

But you have also dared to submit a letter of your own to be read, a letter written about your mother in outrageously disrespectful, abusive, and unseemly language, written too at a time when you were still being brought up under her loving care. This letter you sent secretly to Pontianus, and you have now produced it to avoid the reproach of having sinned only once and to make sure that he could catch a glance of your good deed! Poor fool, do you not realize that your uncle permitted you to do this, that he might clear himself in public estimation by using your letter as proof that even before you migrated to his house, even at the time when you caressed your mother with false words of love, you were already as cunning as any fox and devoid of all filial affection?

But I cannot bring myself to believe Aemilianus such a fool as to think that the letter of a mere boy, who is also one of my accusers, could seriously tell against me.

There is also that forged letter by which they attempted to prove that I beguiled Pudentilla with flattery. I never wrote it and the forgery is not even plausible. What need did I have of flattery, if I put my trust in magic? And how did they secure possession of that letter which must, as is usual in such affairs, have been sent to Pudentilla by some confidential servant? Why, again, should I write in such faulty words, such barbarous language, I whom my accusers admit to be quite at home in Greek? And why should I seek to seduce her by flattery so absurd and coarse? They themselves admit that I write amatory verse with sufficient sprightliness and skill. The explanation is obvious to everyone; it is this: he who could not read the letter which Pudentilla wrote in Greek altogether too refined for his comprehension, found it easier to read this letter and set it off to greater advantage because it was his own.

One more point and I shall have said enough about the letters. Pudentilla, after writing in jest and irony those words

'Come then, while I am yet in my senses,' sent for her sons and her daughter-in-law and lived with them for about two months. I beg this most dutiful of sons to tell us whether he then noticed his mother's alleged madness to have affected for the worse either her words or her deeds. Let him deny that she showed the utmost shrewdness in her examination of the accounts of the bailiffs, grooms, and shepherds, that she earnestly warned his brother Pontianus to be on his guard against the designs of Rufinus, that she rebuked him severely for having freely published the letter she had sent him without having read it honestly as it was written! Let him deny that, after what I have just related to you, his mother married me in her country house, as had been agreed some time previously!

The reason for our decision to be married by preference at her country house not far from Oea was to avoid a fresh concourse of citizens demanding largesse. It was but a short time before that Pudentilla had distributed 50,000 sesterces to the people on the occasion of Pontianus' marriage and this boy's assumption of the garb of manhood. We also wished to avoid the frequent and wearisome dinner-parties which custom generally imposes on newly-married couples. This is the whole reason, Aemilianus, why our marriage contract was signed not in the town but at a country house in the neighbourhood — to avoid squandering another 50,000 sesterces and to escape dining in your company or at your house. Is that sufficient?

I must say that I am surprised that you object so strongly to the country house, considering that you spend most of your time in the country. The Julian marriage-law nowhere contains a clause such as 'no man shall wed in a country house.' Indeed, if you would know the truth, it is of far better omen for the expectation of offspring that one should marry one's wife in a country house in preference to the town, on rich soil in preference to barren ground, on the greensward of the meadow rather than the pavement of the market-place. She that would be a mother should marry in the very bosom of her mother, among the standing crops, on the fruitful ploughland, or she should lie beneath the elm that weds the vine, on the very lap of mother earth, among the springing herbage, the trailing vine-shoots and the budding trees. I may add that the metaphor in the line so well known in comedy

that in the furrow children true be sown

bears out this view most strongly. The ancient Romans also, such as Quintius, Serranus and many others, were offered not only wives but consulships and dictatorships in the open field. On such an abundant topic, I will restrain myself for fear of gratifying you by my praise of country life.

As to Pudentilla's age, concerning which you lied so boldly as to assert that she had married at the age of sixty, I will reply in a few words. It is not necessary to speak at length in discussing a matter where the truth is so obvious.

Her father acknowledged her for his daughter in the usual fashion; the documents in which he did so are preserved partly in the public record office, partly in his house. Here they are before your very eyes. Please hand the documents to Aemilianus. Let him examine the linen strip that bears the seal; let him recognize the seal stamped upon it, let him read the names of the consuls for the year, let him count up the years. He gave her sixty years. Let him bring out the total at fifty-five, admitting that he lied and gave her five too many. Nay, that is hardly enough. I will deal yet more liberally with him. He gave Pudentilla such a number of years that I will reward him by returning ten. Mezentius has been wandering with Ulysses; let him at least prove that she is fifty.

To cut the matter short, as I am dealing with an accuser who is used to multiplying by four, I will multiply five years by four and subtract twenty years at one fell swoop. I beg you, Maximus, to order the number of consuls since her birth to be reckoned. If I am not mistaken, you will find that Pudentilla has barely passed her fortieth year. The insolent audacity of this falsehood! Twenty years' exile would be a worthy punishment for such mendacity! Your fiction has added a good half to the sum, your fabrication is one and a half times the size of the original. Had you said thirty years when you ought to have said ten, it might have been supposed that you had made a slip in the gesture used for your calculation, that you had placed your fore-finger against the middle joint of your thumb, when you should have made them form a circle. But whereas the gesture indicating forty is the simplest of all such gestures, for you have merely to hold out the palm of your hand — you have increased the number by half as much again. There is no room for an erroneous gesture; the only possible hypothesis is that, believing Pudentilla to be thirty, you got your total by adding up the number of consuls, two to each year.

I have done with this. I come now to the very heart of the accusation, to the actual motive for the use of magic. I ask Rufinus and Aemilianus to answer me and tell me — even assuming that I am the most consummate magician — what I had to gain by persuading Pudentilla to marry me by means of my love philtres and my incantations.

I am well aware that many persons, when accused of some crime or other, even if it has been shown that there was some real motive for the offence, have amply cleared themselves of guilt by this one line of defence, that the whole record of their lives renders the suspicion of such a crime incredible and that even though there may have been strong temptation to sin, the mere fact of the existence of the temptation should not be counted against them. We have no right to assume that everything that might have been done actually has been done. Circumstances may alter; the one true guide is a man's character; the one sure indication that a charge should be rejected or believed is the fact that through all his life the accused has set his face towards vice or virtue as the case may be.

I might with the utmost justice put in such a plea for myself, but I waive my right in your favour, and shall think that I have made out but a poor case for myself, if I merely clear myself of all your charges, if I merely show that there exists not the slightest ground for suspecting me of sorcery. Consider what confidence in my innocence and what contempt of you is implied by my conduct. If you can discover one trivial reason that might have led me to woo Pudentilla for the sake of some personal advantage, if you can prove that I have made the very slightest profit out of my marriage, I am ready to be any magician you please — the great Carmendas himself or Damigeron or Moses, or Jannes or Apollobex or Dardanus himself or any sorcerer of note from the time of Zoroaster and Ostanes till now.

See, Maximus, what a disturbance they have raised, merely because I have mentioned a few magicians by name. What am I to do with men so stupid and uncivilized? Shall I proceed to prove to you that I have come across these names and many more in the course of my study of distinguished authors in the public libraries? Or shall I argue that the knowledge of the names of sorcerers is one thing, participation in their art another, and that it is not tantamount to confessing a crime to have one's brain well stored with learning and a memory retentive of its erudition? Or shall I take what is far the best course and, relying on your learning, Maximus, and your perfect erudition, disdain to reply to the accusations of these stupid and uncultivated fellows? Yes, that is what I will do. I will not care a straw for what they may think. I will go on with the argument on which I had entered and will show that I had no motive for seducing Pudentilla into marriage by the use of love philtres. My accusers have gone out of their way to make disparaging remarks both about her age and her appearance; they have denounced me for desiring such a wife from motives of greed and robbing her of her vast and magnificent dowry at the very outset of our wedded life.

I do not intend to weary you Maximus, with a long reply on these points. There is no need for words from me, our deeds of settlement will speak more eloquently than I can do. From them you will see that both in my provision for the future and in my action at the time my conduct was precisely the opposite of that which they have attributed to me, inferring my rapacity from their own. You will see that Pudentilla's dowry was small, considering her wealth, and was made over to me as a trust, not as a gift, and moreover that the marriage only took place on this condition that if my wife should die without leaving me any children, the dowry should go to her sons Pontianus and Pudens, while if at her death she should leave me one son or daughter, half of the dowry was to go to the offspring of the second marriage, the remainder to the sons of the first.

This, as I say, I will prove from the actual deed of settlement. It may be that Aemilianus will still refuse to believe that the total sum recorded is only 30,000 sesterces, and that the reveNion of this sum is given by the settlement to Pudentilla's sons. Take the deeds into your own hands, give them to Rufinus who incited you to this accusation. Let him read them, let him blush for his arrogant temper and his pretentious beggary. He is poor and ill-clad and borrowed 400,000 sesterces to dower his daughter, while Pudentilla, a woman of fortune, was content with 300,000, and her husband, who has often refused the hand of the richest heiresses, is also content with this trifling dowry, a mere nominal sum. He cares for nothing save his wife and counts harmony with his spouse and great love as his sole treasure, his only wealth.

Who that had the least experience of life, would dare to pass any censure if a widow of inconsiderable beauty and considerable age, being desirous of marriage, had by the offer of a large dowry and easy conditions invited a young man, who, whether as regards appearance, character or wealth, was no despicable match, to become her husband? A beautiful maiden, even though she is poor, is amply dowered. For she brings to her husband a fresh untainted spirit, the charm of her beauty, the unblemished glory of her prime. The very fact that she is a maiden is rightly and deservedly regarded by all husbands as the strongest recommendation. For whatever else you receive as your wife's dowry you can, when it pleases you and if you desire to feel yourself under no further obligation, repay in full just as you received it; you can count back the money, restore the slaves, leave the howe, abandon the estates. Virginity only, once it has been given, can never be repaid; it is the one portion of the dowry that remains irrevocably with the husband.

A widow on the other hand, if divorced, leaves you as she came. She brings you nothing that she cannot ask back, she has been another's and is certainly far from tractable to your wishes; she looks suspiciously on her new home, while you regard her with suspicion because she has already been parted from one husband: if it was by death she lost her husband, the evil omen of her ill-starred union minimizes her attractions, while, if she left him by divorce, she possesses one of two faults: either she was so intolerable that she was divorced by her husband, or so insolent as to divorce him. It is for reasons of this kind among others that widows offer a larger dowry to attract suitors for their hands. Pudentilla would have done the same had she not found a philosopher indifferent to her dowry.

Consider. If I had desired her from motives of avarice, what could have been more profitable to me in my attempt to make myself master in her house than the dissemination of strife between mother and sons, the alienation of her children from her affections, so that I might have unfettered and supreme control over her loneliness? Such would have been, would it not, the action of the brigand you pretend me to be.

But as a matter of fact I did all I could to promote, to restore and foster quiet and harmony and family affection, and not only abstained from sowing fresh feuds, but utterly extinguished those already in existence. I urged my wife — whose whole fortune according to my accusers I had by this time devoured — I urged her and finally persuaded her, when her sons demanded back the money of which I spoke above, to pay over the whole sum at once in the shape of farms, at a low valuation and at the price suggested by themselves, and further to surrender from her own private property certain exceedingly fertile lands, a large house richly decorated, a great quantity of wheat, barley, wine and oil, and other fruits of the earth, together with not less than four hundred slaves and a large number of valuable cattle. Finally I persuaded her to abandon all claims on the portion she had given them and to give them good hopes of one day coming into the rest of the property. All these concessions I extorted from

Pudentilla with difficulty and against her will — I have her leave to tell the whole story as it happened — I wrung them from her by my urgent entreaty, though she was angry and reluctant. I reconciled the mother with her sons, and began my career as a step-father by enriching my step-sons with a large sum of money.

All Oea was aware of this. Every one execrated Rufinus and extolled mg conduct.

Pontianus together with his very inferior brother had come to visit us, before his mother had completed her donation. He fell at our feet and implored us to forgive and forget all his past offences; he wept, kissed our hands and expressed his penitence for listening to Rufinus and others like him. He also most humbly begged me to make his excuses to the most honourable Lollianus Avitus to whom I had recommended him not long before when he was beginning the study of oratory. He had discovered that I had written to Avitus a few days previously a full account of all that had happened. I granted him this request also and gave him a letter with which he set off to Carthage, where Lollianus Avitus, the term of his proconsulate having nearly expired, was awaiting your arrival, Maximus. After reading my letters he congratulated Pontianus with the exquisite courtesy which always characterizes him for having so soon rectified his error and entrusted him with a reply. Ah! what learning! what wit! what grace and charm dwelt in that reply! Only a 'good man and an orator' could have written it.

I know, Maximus, that you will readily give a hearing to this letter. Indeed, if it is to be read, I will recite it myself. Give me Avitus' letter. That I should have received it has always flattered me. Today it shall do more than flatter, it shall save me! You may let the water-clock continue, for I would gladly read and re-read the letter of that excellent man to the third and fourth time at the cost of any amount of the time allowed me.

I know that after reading this letter I should bring my speech to a close. For what ampler commendation, what purer testimony could I produce in my support, what more eloquent advocacy? I have in the course of my life listened with rapt attention to many eloquent Romans, but never have I admired any so much as Avitus. There is in my opinion no one living of any attainments or promise in oratory who would not far sooner be Avitus, if he compares him with himself impartially and without envy. For practically all the different excellencies of oratory are united in him. Whatever speech Avitus composes will be found so absolutely perfect and complete in all respects that it would satisfy Cato by its dignity, Laelius with its smoothness, Gracchus with its energy, Caesar with its warmth, Hortensius with its arrangement, Calvus with its point, Sallust with its economy and Cicero with its wealth of rhetoric. In fact, not to go through all his merits, if you were to hear Avitus, you would wish nothing added, withdrawn or altered of anything that he says.

I see, Maximus, with what pleasure you listen to the recital of the virtues which you recognize your friend Avitus to possess. Your courtesy invited me to say a few words about him. But I will not trespass on your kindness so far as to permit myself to commence a discourse on his extraordinary virtues at this period of the case. It is wearing to its end and my powers are almost exhausted. I will rather reserve the praise of Avitus' virtues for some day when my time is free and my powers unimpaired.

Now, I grieve to say, it is my duty to turn from the description of so great a man to discuss these pestilent fellows here. Do you dare then, Aemilianus, to match yourself against Avitus? Will you attack with accusations of magic and the black art him whom Avitus describes as a good man, and whose disposition he praises so warmly in his letter? Or do you have greater reason to be vexed at my forcing my way into Pudentilla's house and pillaging her goods than Pontianus would have had, Pontianus, who not only in my presence but even before Avitus in my absence, made amends for the strife of a few days that had sprung up between us at your instigation, and expressed his gratitude to me in the presence of so great a man?

Suppose I had read a report of what took place in Avitus' presence instead of reading merely his letter. What is there in the whole affair that could give you or anyone else a handle for accusing me? Pontianus himself considered himself in my debt for the money given him by his mother; Pontianus rejoiced with the utmost sincerity in his good fortune in having me for his stepfather. Ah! would that he had returned from Carthage safe and sound! Or since it was not fated that that should be, would that you, Rufinus, had not poisoned his judgement at the last! What gratitude he would have expressed to me either personally or in his will! However, as things are, I beg you, Maximus, — it will not take long — to allow the reading of these letters full of expressions of respect and affection for myself, which he sent me, some of them from Carthage, some as he drew near on his homeward journey, some written while he still enjoyed his health, and some when the sickness was already upon him. Thus his brother, my accuser, will realize how in everything he is running a Minerva's course with his brother, a man of blessed memory.

Did you hear the phrases which your brother Pontianus used in speaking of me? He called me his father, his master, his instructor not only on various occasions in his lifetime but actually on his deathbed. I might follow this by producing similar letters from you, if I thought that the delay thus caused would be worth while. But I should prefer to produce your brother's recent will, unfinished though it may be, in which he made most dutiful and respectful mention of myself. But Rufinus never allowed this will to be drawn up or completed owing to his chagrin at the loss of the inheritance which he had regarded in the light of a rich payment for his daughter's embraces during the few months in which he was Pontianus' father-in-law. He had further consulted certain Chaldean soothsayers as to what profit his daughter, whom he regarded in the light of an investment, would bring him in. They, I am told, prophesied truly — would they had not — that her first husband would die in a few months. The rest of the prophecy dealing with the inheritance was as usual fabricated to suit the debires of their client.

But Rufinus gaped for his prey in vain like a wild beast that has gone blind. For Pontianus not only did not leave Rufinus' daughter as his heir — he had discovered her evil character —

but he did not even make her a respectable legacy. He left her by way of insult linen to the value of 200 denarii, to show that he had not forgotten or ignored her, but that he set this value on her as an expression of his resentment. As his heirs — in this just as in the former will which has been read aloud — he appointed his mother and his brother, against whom, mere boy as he is, Rufinus is, as you see, bringing his old artillery into play: I refer to his daughter. He thrusts her upon his embraces although she is considerably his elder and but a brief while ago was his brother's wife.

Pudens was so captivated and possessed by the charms of that harlot and by the beguiling words of the pander, her father, that the moment his brother had breathed his last, he left his mother and migrated to his uncle's house. The design was to facilitate the carrying out of the schemes already afoot by removing him from our influence. For Aemilianus is backing Rufinus and desires his success. Ah! Thank you! You rightly remind me that this excellent uncle has hopes of his own mixed up in this affair, for he knows that if this boy dies intestate he will be his heir-at-law, whatever he may be in point of equity. I wish I had not let this slip. I am a man of great self-control and it is not my way to blurt out openly the silent suspicions that must have occurred to every one. You did wrong in suggesting this point to me!

But to be frank, if you will have the truth, many have been wondering at the sudden affection which you, Aemilianus, have begun to show for this boy since the death of his brother Pontianus, whereas formerly you were such a stranger to him that frequently, even when you met him, you failed to recognize the face of your brother's son. But now you show yourself so patient towards him, you so spoil him by your indulgence and grant his every whim to such an extent that your conduct makes the more suspicious think their suspicions well grounded. You took him from us a mere boy and straightway gave him the garb of manhood. While he was under our guardianship, he used to go to school: now he has bidden a long farewell to study and betaken himself to the delights of the tavern. He despises serious friends, and, boy as he is, spends his tender years in revelling with the most abandoned youths among harlots and wine-cups. He rules your house, orders your slaves, directs your banquets. He is frequently seen in the gladiatorial school and there — as a boy of position should! — he learns from the keeper of the school the names of the gladiators, the fights they have fought, the wounds they have received. He never speaks any language save Punic, and though he may occasionally use a Greek word picked up from his mother, he neither will nor can speak Latin. You heard, Maximus, a little while ago, you heard my step-son — oh! the shame of it! — the brother of that eloquent young fellow Pontianus, hardly able to stammer out single syllables, when you asked him whether his mother had given himself and his brother the gifts which, as I told you just now, she actually gave them with my hearty support.

I call you, therefore, Claudius Maximus, and you, gentlemen, his assessors, and you that with me stand before this tribunal, to bear witness that this boy's disgraceful falling away in morals is due to his uncle here and that candidate for the privilege of becoming his father-in-law, and that I shall henceforth count it a blessing that such a step-son has lifted the burden of superintending him from my shoulders, and that from this day forth I will never intercede for him with his mother.

For recently — I had almost forgotten to mention it — when Pudentilla, who had fallen ill after the death of her son Pontianus, was writing her will, I had a prolonged struggle to prevent her disinheriting this boy on account of the outrageous insult and injury he had inflicted on her. I prayed her with the utmost earnestness to erase that most important clause, which, I can assure you, she had already written, every word of it! Finally, I even threatened to leave her, if she refused to accede to my request, and begged her to grant me this boon, to conquer her wicked son by kindness, and to save me from all the ill feeling which her action would create. I did not desist till she complied.

I regret that I should have taken away this point of concern from Aemilianus and showed him such an unexpected thing.

Look, Maximus, see how confused he is at hearing this, see how he casts his eyes upon the ground. He had not unnaturally expected something very different. He knew that my wife was angry with her son on account of his insolent behaviour and that she returned my devotion. He had reason also for fear in regard to myself; for anyone else, even if like myself he had been above coveting the inheritance, would gladly have seen so undutiful a step-son punished. It was this anxiety above all others that spurred them on to accuse me. Their own avarice led them falsely to conjecture that the whole inheritance had been left to me. As far as the past is concerned, I will dispel your fears on that point. I was proof against the temptation both of enriching myself and of revenging myself. I— a step-father, mind you — contended for my wicked step-son with his mother, as a father might contend against a stepmother in the interests of a virtuous son; nor did I rest satisfied till, with a perfectly extravagant sense of fairness, I had restrained my good wife's lavish generosity towards myself.

Give me the will which was made in the interests of so unfilial a son by his mother. Each word of it was preceded by an entreaty from myself, whom my accusers speak of as a mere robber. Order the tablets to be broken open, Maximus. You will find that her son is the heir, that I get nothing save some trifling complimentary legacy inserted to avoid the non-appearance of my name, the husband's name, mark you, in my wife's will, supposing she succumbed to any of the ills to which this flesh is heir. Take up your mother's will. You are right, in one respect it is undutiful. She excludes her devoted husband from the inheritance in favour of her most unfilial son? Nay, it is not her son to whom she leaves her fortune; she leaves it rather to the greedy Aemilianus and the matchmaking Rufinus and that drunken gang, that hang about you and prey upon you.

Take it, o best of sons! Lay aside your mother's love-letters for a while and read her will instead. If she ever wrote anything while not in her right mind, you will find it here, nor will you have to go far to find it. 'Let Sicinius Pudens, my son, be my heir.' I admit it! he who reads this, will think it insanity. Is this same son your heir, who at his own brother's funeral attempted with the help of a gang of the most abandoned youths to shut you out of the house which you yourself had given him, who is so deeply and bitterly incensed to find that his brother left you co-heir with himself, who hastened to desert you when you were plunged in grief and mourning, and fled from your bosom to Aemilianus and Rufinus, who afterwards uttered many insults against you to your face, and manufactured others with the help of his uncle, who has dragged your name through the law-courts, has attempted by using your own letters publicly to besmirch your fair fame, and has accused upon a capital charge the husband of your choice, with whom, as Pudens himself objected, you were madly in love!

Open the will, my good boy, open it, I beg you. You will find it easier then to prove your mother's insanity. Why do you draw back? Why do you refuse to look at it, now that you are free from all anxiety about the inheritance of your mother's fortune?

He may do as he likes, Maximus, but for my part I cast these tablets at your feet and call you to witness that henceforth I shall show greater indifference as to what Pudentilla may write in her will. He may approach his mother himself for the future; he has made it impossible for me to plead for him again. He is now a man and his own master; henceforth let him himself dictate to his mother the terms of an unpalatable will, himself smooth away her anger. He who can plead in court, will be able to plead with his mother.

I am more than satisfied not only to have refuted the miscellaneous accusations brought against myself, but also to have utterly swept away the hateful charge on which the whole trial is based, the charge of having attempted to secure the inheritance for myself.

I will bring one final proof to show the falsity of that last charge before I bring my speech to a close. I wish to pass nothing over in silence. You asserted that I bought a most excellent farm in my own name, but with a large sum of money which belonged to my wife. I say that a tiny property was bought for 60,000 sesterces, and bought not by me but by Pudentilla in her own name, that Pudentilla's name is in the deed of sale, and that the taxes paid on the land are paid in the name of Pudentilla. The honourable Coninus Celer, the state treasurer to whom the tax is paid, is here in court. Cassius Longinus also is present, my wife's guardian and trustee, a man of the loftiest and most irreproachable character. I cannot speak of him save with the deepest respect. Ask him, Maximus, what was the purchase which he authorized, and what was the trifling sum for which this wealthy lady bought her little estate.

Is it as I said? Is my name ever mentioned in the deed of sale? Is the price paid for this trifling property such as should excite any prejudice against me, or did my wife give me even so much as this small gift?

What is there left, Aemilianus, that in your opinion I have failed to refute? What had I to gain by my magic that should lead me to attempt to win Pudentilla by love-philtres? What had I to gain from her? A small dowry instead of a large one? Truly my incantations were miraculous. That she should refund her dowry to her sons rather than leave it in my possession? What magic can surpass this? That she should at my exhortation present the bulk of her property to her sons and leave me nothing, although before her marriage with myself she had shown them no special generosity? What a criminal we of love-philtres! Or perhaps I had better call it a generous action which has not received its deserts! By her will, which she drew up in a fit of violent irritation against her son, she leaves as her heir that same son with whom she had quarrelled, rather than myself to whom she was devoted! For all my incantations it was only with difficulty that I persuaded her to this.

Suppose that you were pleading your case, not before Claudius Maximus, a man of the utmost fairness and unswerving justice, but before a judge of depraved morals and of ferocious temper, one in fact who naturally inclined to the side of the accuser and was only too ready to condemn the accused! Give him some hint to follow! Give him even the slightest reasonable opportunity for declaring in your favour! At least invent something, devise some suitable reply to questions such as have been put to you.

Nay, since every action must necessarily have some motive, answer me this, you who say that Apuleius tried to influence Pudentilla's heart by magical charms, answer me this! What did he seek to get from her by so doing? Was he in love with her beauty? You say not! Did he covet her wealth? The evidence of the marriage settlement denies it, the evidence of the deed of gift denies it, the evidence of the will denies it! It shows not only that I did not court the generosity of my wife, but that I even repulsed it with some severity. What other motive can you allege? Why are you struck dumb? Why this silence? What has become of that ferocious utterance with which you opened the indictment, couched in the name of my step-son? 'This is the man, most excellent Maximus, whom I have resolved to indict before you.'

Why did you not add 'He whom I indict is my teacher, my step-father, my mediator'? But how did you proceed? 'He is guilty of the most palpable and numerous sorceries.' Produce one of these many sorceries or at least some doubtful instance from those which you style so palpable.

Nay, see whether I cannot reply to your various charges with two words to each. 'You clean your teeth.' Excusable cleanliness. 'You look into mirrors.' Philosophers should. 'You write verse.' 'Tis permitted. 'You examine fish.' Following Aristotle. 'You worship a piece of wood.' So Plato. 'You marry a wife.' Obeying law. 'She is older than you.' Nothing commoner. 'You married for money.' Take the marriage-settlement, remember the deed of gift, read the will!

If I have rebutted all their charges, word by word, if I have refuted all their slanders, if I am beyond reproach, not only as regards their accusations but also as regards their vulgar abuse, if I have done nothing to impair the honour of philosophy, which is dearer to me than my own safety, but on the contrary have smitten my adversary hip and thigh and vanquished him at all points, if all my contentions are true, I can await your estimate of my character with the same confidence with which I await the exercise of your power; for I regard it as less serious and less terrible to be condemned by the proconsul than to incur the disapproval of so good and so perfect a man.

www.ingramcontent.com/pod-product-compliance
Lightning Source LLC
Chambersburg PA
CBHW071741090426
42738CB00011B/2535